Public Attitudes Toward Risk-Based Pricing and Risk-Sharing in Insurance

LLOYD DIXON, JAMES M. ANDERSON

SOCIAL AND ECONOMIC WELL-BEING

For more information on this publication, visit **www.rand.org/t/RRA2872-1**.

About RAND

RAND is a research organization that develops solutions to public policy challenges to help make communities throughout the world safer and more secure, healthier and more prosperous. RAND is nonprofit, nonpartisan, and committed to the public interest. To learn more about RAND, visit www.rand.org.

Research Integrity

Our mission to help improve policy and decisionmaking through research and analysis is enabled through our core values of quality and objectivity and our unwavering commitment to the highest level of integrity and ethical behavior. To help ensure our research and analysis are rigorous, objective, and nonpartisan, we subject our research publications to a robust and exacting quality-assurance process; avoid both the appearance and reality of financial and other conflicts of interest through staff training, project screening, and a policy of mandatory disclosure; and pursue transparency in our research engagements through our commitment to the open publication of our research findings and recommendations, disclosure of the source of funding of published research, and policies to ensure intellectual independence. For more information, visit www.rand.org/about/research-integrity.

RAND's publications do not necessarily reflect the opinions of its research clients and sponsors.

Published by the RAND Corporation, Santa Monica, Calif.
© 2024 RAND Corporation
RAND® is a registered trademark.

Library of Congress Cataloging-in-Publication Data is available for this publication.

ISBN: 978-1-9774-1380-2

Cover image: photoman | Getty Images

About This Report

Insurance is an important societal mechanism that helps allocate costs of various risks. The allocation will depend on how the insurance is priced. At one end of the spectrum, insurance can be priced without restriction based on an insurer's best estimate of the risk posed by the insured individual. At the other, the collective costs can be pooled so that individuals pay the same regardless of their risk. In the latter case, low-risk policyholders cross-subsidize high-risk policyholders. Critical to understanding pressures to price at various points across this spectrum are public attitudes toward pricing based on individual risk factors and cross-subsidization. Remarkably, we know very little about our collective attitudes toward sharing and spreading risk. To help fill this gap, this report addresses the following research questions:

- In what contexts does the public support insurance premiums that are based on individual risk factors?
- How much are people willing to pay to subsidize the premiums of higher-risk policyholders?
- How does support of pricing based on individual risk factors vary across demographic groups?

The RAND Kenneth R. Feinberg Center for Catastrophic Risk Management and Compensation

The Feinberg Center, part of the Justice Policy Program within RAND Social and Economic Well-Being, seeks to identify and promote laws, programs, and institutions that reduce the adverse social and economic effects of natural and manmade catastrophes by improving incentives to reduce future losses; providing just compensation to those suffering losses while appropriately allocating liability to responsible parties; helping affected individuals, businesses, and communities to recover quickly; and avoiding unnecessary legal, administrative, and other transaction costs.

Questions or comments about this report should be sent to the project leader, Lloyd Dixon (dixon@rand.org). For more information about the Feinberg Center, see www.rand.org/well-being/justice-policy/centers/catastrophic-risk-management.html or contact the director at ccrmc@rand.org.

Institute for Civil Justice

The RAND Institute for Civil Justice (ICJ) is dedicated to improving the civil justice system by supplying policymakers and the public with rigorous and nonpartisan research. Its studies identify trends in litigation and inform policy choices concerning liability, compensation, regulation, risk management, and insurance. The Institute builds on a long tradition of RAND research characterized by an interdisciplinary, empirical approach to public policy issues and rigorous standards of quality, objectivity, and independence. ICJ research is supported by pooled grants from a range of sources, including corporations, trade and professional associations, individuals, government agencies, and private foundations. All its reports are subject to peer review and disseminated widely to policymakers, practitioners in law and business, other researchers, and the public. The ICJ is part of the Justice Policy Program within RAND Social and Economic Well-Being. The program focuses on such topics as access to justice, policing, corrections, drug policy, and court system reform, as well as other policy concerns pertaining to public safety and criminal and civil justice. For more information, email justicepolicy@rand.org.

Funding

Funding for this research was provided by the generous contributions of the RAND Institute for Civil Justice Advisory Board and the RAND Kenneth R. Feinberg Center for Catastrophic Risk Management and Compensation Advisory Board.

Acknowledgments

Excellent peer reviews of the draft report were provided by Misha Dworsky, RAND senior economist, and Douglas Heller, director of insurance at the Consumer Federation of America. Valuable comments were provided by the RAND Institute for Civil Justice and Feinberg Center advisory boards. Helpful suggestions about survey design were provided by David Grant, principal investigator of the RAND American Life Panel; Andrew Parker, senior behavior scientist at RAND and co-director of the RAND Center for Decision Making under Uncertainty; and Bruce Bender, of Bender Consulting Services. We thank Karen Edwards, who was the general manager of the RAND American Life Panel at the time of this study, for managing the coding of the survey, the survey fielding, and the preparation of the data. We also thank Amy Nicoletti for her very skillful work editing the document. James Anderson would like to thank George Priest and Guido Calabresi for sparking his long-standing interest in risk perception, insurance regulation, and the costs of accidents.

Summary

Insurance is an important societal mechanism that helps allocate costs of various risks. The allocation will depend on how the insurance is priced. At one end of the spectrum, insurance can be priced without restriction based on an insurer's best estimate of the risk posed by the insured individual. At the other, the collective costs can be pooled so that individuals pay the same regardless of their risk. In the latter case, low-risk policyholders cross-subsidize high-risk policyholders. Critical to understanding pressures to price at various points across this spectrum are public attitudes toward pricing based on individual risk factors and cross-subsidization. Remarkably, very little is known about collective attitudes toward sharing and spreading risk. To help fill this gap, this report addresses the following research questions:

- In what contexts does the public support insurance premiums that are based on individual risk factors?
- How much are people willing to pay to subsidize the premiums of higher-risk policyholders?
- How does support of pricing based on individual risk factors vary across demographic groups?

Approach

Figure S.1 illustrates the spectrum of pricing approaches we examined in this study. At one end of the spectrum is risk-based pricing. *Risk-based pricing* reflects pricing based on the full observable difference in risk across policyholder groups. At the other end of spectrum is full risk-sharing. We define *full risk-sharing* as situations in which all policyholders pay the same premium regardless of risk. Lower-risk policyholders do not cross-subsidize higher-risk policyholders when pricing is risk-based, and cross-subsidies increase as one moves along the spectrum from risk-based pricing to full risk-sharing.

FIGURE S.1

Spectrum of Pricing Approaches Considered in This Study

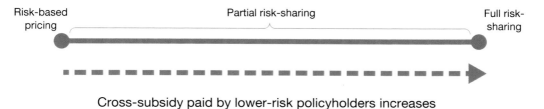

Risk-based pricing   Partial risk-sharing   Full risk-sharing

Cross-subsidy paid by lower-risk policyholders increases

We refer to points on the pricing spectrum between risk-based pricing and full risk-sharing as *partial risk-sharing*. We also distinguish between full risk-sharing and all other points on the pricing spectrum. *Pricing based on individual risk factors* refers to situations in which the premiums charged to higher-risk policyholders are greater than those charged to lower-risk policyholders, but the difference does not necessarily reflect the full difference in risk. Risk-based pricing is thus a special case of pricing based on individual risk factors.

To gauge public attitudes toward full risk-sharing, partial risk-sharing, and risk-based pricing, we surveyed a representative sample of the U.S. adult population. We asked survey respondents two types of questions. In the first set of questions, participants were asked whether policyholders should pay more for insurance based on specific risk factors. In all cases, survey respondents were directed to assume that the risk factor in question is associated with higher losses. This first type of question provides information on whether the public supports pricing based on individual risk factors. However, it does not provide information on the degree to which prices should reflect the underlying risk, and survey respondents might not consider who pays the subsidy. The second type of survey question addresses these limitations. To do so, we presented survey respondents with three or four different insurance rate plans in various settings and asked respondents to rank the plans in order of preference. At one extreme, all policyholders pay the same premium regardless of their individual risk (full risk-sharing), and at the other, premiums are risk-based. In the second type of question, low-risk policyholders usually pay any subsidies (low-risk policyholders cross-subsidize the premiums of high-risk policyholders), although survey respondents are not explicitly alerted to this fact. A potential limitation of our survey approach is that the survey respondents do not actually pay the subsidies, and thus their support for subsidies could be lower in real-world situations.

The survey was conducted in December 2021 and January 2022, and 867 individuals completed the survey (71.3-percent response rate). Survey responses were weighted to be representative of the U.S. adult population.

Findings

Support for Risk-Based Pricing Varies Considerably Across Insurance Settings

We found that the support for pricing based on individual risk factors depends on the risk in question. In general, there is less support for pricing based on individual risk factors when the risk is perceived to be outside the policyholder's control. In contrast, pricing based on individual risk factors is more acceptable if policyholders have more control over the risk. For example, among the U.S. adult population, only 4 percent and 2 percent support or strongly support, respectively, higher health insurance premiums for people with certain genetic disorders (see top row of Figure S.2). Conversely, a solid majority support or strongly support higher premiums for people who use illegal drugs (last row of Figure S.2). We saw similar results for term life insurance.

FIGURE S.2

Public Support for Higher Health Insurance Premiums by Risk Factor

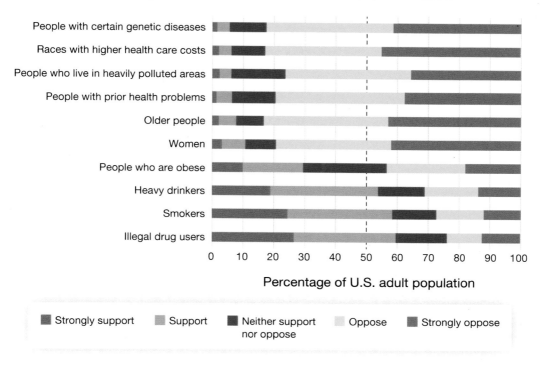

SOURCE: Authors' analysis of survey responses.

In the automobile (hereafter, auto) insurance setting, more than 80 percent support higher premiums for drivers with more speeding tickets (see bottom row of Figure S.3). However, when survey respondents were directed to assume that low credit scores were associated with higher accident rates, few supported higher insurance premiums for this group—perhaps because respondents did not believe that the link between driving behavior and credit scores is sufficiently direct or felt that credit scores are often driven by factors outside the individual's control.

FIGURE S.3

Public Support for Higher Auto Insurance Premiums by Risk Factor

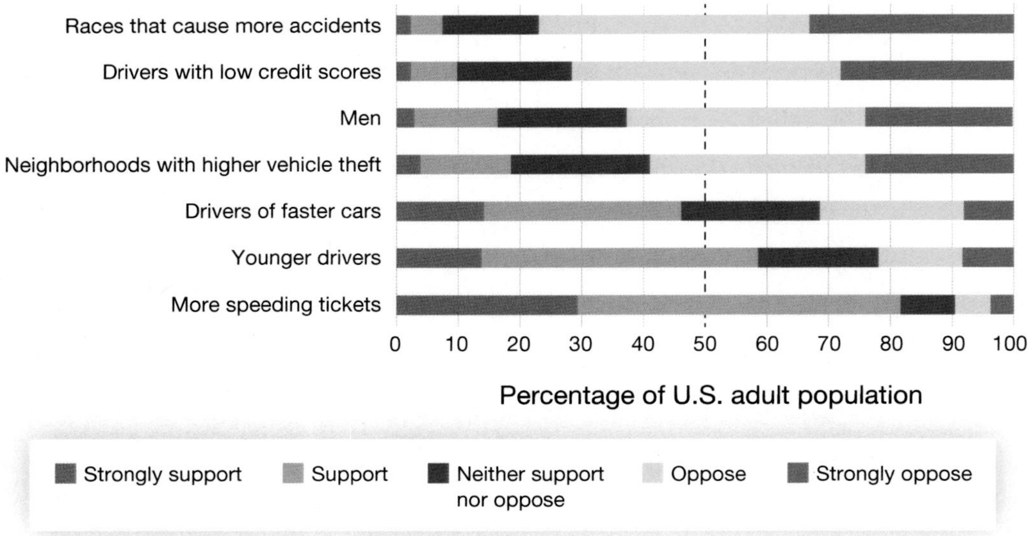

SOURCE: Authors' analysis of survey responses.

Our findings for flood insurance evidenced significant support for spreading the cost of risk in a number of circumstances. Although approximately two-thirds of the population supports the general concept that flood insurance premiums should be higher for homes at higher flood risk (see bottom row of Figure S.4), support falls below 50 percent when the particular details of the situation are considered. If the home is at higher risk but the homeowner has limited assets and low income, the percentage of the population supporting or strongly supporting higher premiums drops to less than 40 percent. If the higher risk is due to factors that are beyond the homeowner's control, such as sea level rise or nearby development, support for higher premiums further declines.

FIGURE S.4

Public Support for Higher Flood Insurance Premiums by Risk Factor

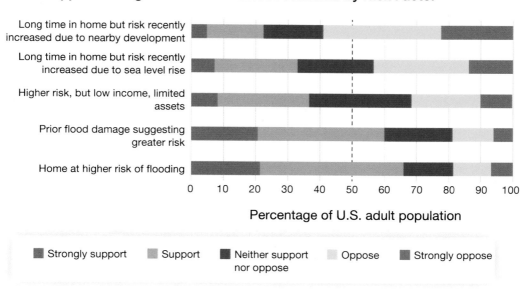

Percentage of U.S. adult population

■ Strongly support ■ Support ■ Neither support ░ Oppose ■ Strongly oppose
                                   nor oppose

SOURCE: Authors' analysis of survey responses.

Support for Substantial Subsidies Is Considerable

Not only is there limited support for insurance pricing based on individual risk factors in many circumstances, but also people are often willing to pay substantial amounts to support the resulting subsidies. As shown in the penultimate column of Table S.1, 66 percent of the U.S. adult population prefer a rate plan in which low-risk health insurance policyholders each pay an additional $2,000 per year to subsidize the premiums of people with leukemia, increasing the premium paid by low-risk policyholders by 20 percent. Only 10 percent prefer the risk-based rate plan to the other rate plans offered.

More detailed analysis of how respondents ranked the three rating plans allows further insight into the preferred subsidy levels. Under reasonable assumptions about the social welfare functions that respondents use to rank the rating plans, we infer that at least 57 percent of the U.S. adult population would choose a subsidy that increases the premium of low-risk policyholders $1,000 to $2,000 per year. The percentage could be considerably higher, but useful estimates are not possible given the data available.

Public support for subsidies is considerably lower when it is the health care insurance premiums of people who drink heavily that are being subsidized (see last column of Table S.1). In this scenario, somewhat less than one-half of the population (44 percent) prefer the plan with no subsidies. However, there is still considerable support for substantial subsidies for people who drink heavily. In this case, we infer that at least 31 percent of the U.S. adult population prefer a subsidy that increases the premium of people who do not drink heavily $1,000 to $2,000 per year.

TABLE S.1

Preferred Subsidy Levels in a Health Insurance Setting

Rate Plan	Low-Risk Policyholders		High-Risk Policyholders		Percentage of Population Preferring Plan	
	Subsidy Paid ($/policyholder)	Percentage Change in Premium[a]	Subsidy Received ($/policyholder)	Percentage Change in Premium[a]	Leukemia Scenario[a]	Heavy-Drinking Scenario[b]
Risk-based pricing	0	0	0	0	10	44
Partial risk-sharing	1,000	10	10,000	−33	24	20
Full risk-sharing	2,000	20	18,000	−60	66	36

SOURCE: Authors' analysis of survey responses.

[a] Risk-based premium for healthy people is $10,000 per year and $30,000 per year for people with leukemia.

[b] Risk-based premium for people who do not drink heavily is $10,000 per year and $30,000 per year for people who drink heavily.

The findings are similar in a flood insurance setting. More than one-half of the population prefer the pricing plan in which homeowners in low-risk areas pay $500 or $1,000 more to reduce the premiums of homeowners in high-risk areas (combine the last two rows of the last column of Table S.2). In this case, we infer that at least 24 percent of the U.S. adult population prefer a subsidy that increases the premium of low-risk policyholders $500 to $1,000 per year.

When flood insurance premiums increase in high-risk areas due to sea level rise, nearly 70 percent of the population believe that either the federal government should cover the increase or that homeowners in low-risk areas should pay 100 to 300 percent more to subsidize the premiums in high-risk areas.

TABLE S.2

Preferred Subsidy Levels in a Flood Insurance Setting

Rate Plan	Low-Risk Policyholders		High-Risk Policyholders		Percentage of Population Preferring Plan[a]
	Subsidy Paid ($/policyholder per year)	Percentage Change in Premium	Subsidy Received ($/policyholder per year)	Percentage Change in Premium	
Risk-based pricing	0	0	0	0	45
Partial risk-sharing	500	100	500	−20	24
Full risk-sharing	1,000	200	1,000	−40	31

SOURCE: Authors' analysis of survey responses.

[a] The risk-based premium is $500 per year for homes in low-risk areas and $2,500 per year for homes in high-risk areas.

Support for Pricing Based on Individual Risk Factors Varies by Demographic Group

Men tend to be more in favor of linking premiums to individual risk factors than women, holding the other demographic factors considered in the analysis fixed. Older Americans tend to be more in favor of pricing based on individual risk factors than younger Americans. Individuals in higher-income households also are more in favor of linking premiums to risk factors than those in lower-income households. Black respondents, in contrast, are less supportive of pricing based on individual risk factors than White respondents, holding other demographic characteristics constant.

Conclusion

Overall, we find that attitudes toward full risk-sharing, partial risk-sharing, and risk-based pricing vary considerably within the population and across insurance settings. Premiums that vary with individual risk are not popular in many settings, and our results suggest that many people are willing to pay considerable amounts to subsidize the insurance premiums of higher-risk individuals.

Our findings have implications for insurance regulation and the role that insurance can play in mitigating the effects of natural and other hazards. In auto insurance, we find that many commonly used rating factors (e.g., neighborhood, credit score) are broadly unpopular. Our findings in the flood insurance setting help explain the challenges that the Federal Emergency Management Agency faces in moving to risk-based pricing. They also explain the public pressure to exempt certain properties from flood insurance rate increases when those rate increases are due to factors beyond the policyholder's control.

The substantial support for subsidies that we found raises questions about the potential efficacy of relying on insurance to create incentives to mitigate the effects of natural and other hazards. Risk-based premiums, or premiums close to risk-based premiums, can provide incentives to reduce the vulnerability of individuals or property to natural and other hazards. For example, if flood insurance premiums rise to reflect the increased risk from sea level rise, they may encourage homebuyers to buy properties in areas that are less subject to such risk. However, the considerable popular support for substantial subsidies calls into question whether insurance will be able to fulfill its potential to provide appropriate incentives.

Several approaches come to mind to address the apparent mismatch between the theoretical benefits of risk-based prices and public sentiment. First, education may help the public understand some of the drawbacks of subsidies and risk-spreading. This may lead to more support for risk-based pricing and the climate-change risk mitigation strategies that they incentivize. Highlighting some of the apparent unfairness of cross-subsidizing a wealthy waterfront landowner's insurance policy, for example, might shift opinions.

Second, rating plans should be considered that move in the direction of risk-based pricing but address some of the fairness and equity considerations. For example, prices might be set at risk-based rates, but targeted assistance could be provided to low-income households under certain circumstances or over limited periods to reduce the burdens of such rates.

Finally, further research in a number of areas would improve understanding of the public attitudes toward risk-based pricing and their implications for public policy. Areas that deserve further investigation include the following:

- impact of personalizing the scenarios
- impact of providing additional information on risk factors
- difference in attitudes when coverage is mandatory
- factors driving consumer preferences
- more-precise estimates of the subsidies that consumers are willing to pay
- use of laboratory experiments to corroborate findings
- quantitative analysis of the real-world inefficiencies and lost consumer welfare attributable to cross-subsidies.

Contents

Figures and Tables

Figures

Tables

CHAPTER 1

Introduction

Insurance is a critical tool by which society collectively allocates the costs of various risks. The extent to which insurance premiums are based on individual risk factors as opposed to the average risk in the population has important implications for social policy, as well as the functioning of insurance markets. At one end of the spectrum, insurance can be priced, without restriction, based on an insurer's best estimate of the risk posed by the individual insured. At the other, the collective costs can be pooled so that individuals pay the same regardless of their individual risk. In the latter case, low-risk policyholders cross-subsidize high-risk policyholders. In the real world, insurers rarely have perfect information about the true risk posed by the insured, so matching price to risk can never be perfect; nevertheless, insurance regulators and policymakers have important decisions to make about the extent to which they implicitly or explicitly encourage premiums to be based on individual risk factors or the average risk across the population.[1]

Risk-based pricing has important advantages. If insurance premiums are risk-based—that is, if they reflect the expected claim costs during the policy term for the individual policyholder—they can create appropriate incentives to induce behaviors that reduce risk. For example, if a person's automobile (hereafter, auto) insurance premium is based on that individual's driving record, they might drive less often or more carefully to reduce their insurance premium. If premiums are not risk-based but cross-subsidized by other policyholders or subsidized by the government, they can lessen the incentives of parties whose rates are subsidized. So, for example, if a person's auto insurance is not dependent on the number of speeding tickets that individual has received, they might drive more recklessly. This is a version of *moral hazard*.[2] In such situations, insurance may not be an effective tool to induce behaviors that mitigate the effects of climate change and other hazards. Departure from risk-based pricing can also reduce the overall benefits of insurance markets. Raising premiums on low-risk policyholders to cross-subsidize the premiums of high-risk policyholders can cause

---

[1] Kenneth S. Abraham, *Distributing Risk: Insurance, Legal Theory, and Public Policy*, Yale University Press, 1986.

[2] This example focuses on a risk factor that is indicative of risk, not the extent to which insured losses have been higher due to past accidents. Basing premiums on past claims is referred to as *experience rating*. This example also describes an instance where, as we will see, the public generally supports using the factor to indicate risk as opposed to factors that the public views less favorably.

low-risk policyholders to drop their coverage when purchase of insurance is not mandatory or buy less coverage than they would have otherwise. Such adverse selection can reduce the overall benefit generated by the market.[3]

Still, in most insurance markets, it is difficult to perfectly measure individual risk, so almost every insurance market operates at some point on the continuum between perfectly measured risk-based prices and charging everyone the same price. Even if regulators permit it, insurers cannot perfectly observe individual risk, and so insurance pricing is always somewhat of an approximation.

Although risk-based pricing has many desirable characteristics, it may be inconsistent with our collective intuitions about the extent to which risk should be shared. For example, U.S. health insurers are not allowed to charge higher premiums for preexisting conditions in many settings, even though those preexisting conditions can accurately predict claim costs during the policy period.[4] There is thus a trade-off between risk-based premiums and other social objectives that are based on equity, fairness, a sense of community, and the common good.

Critical to understanding pressures for and against these two competing considerations are public attitudes toward risk-based pricing and cross-subsidization in different settings. Public support for risk-sharing could prompt legislators and regulators to constrain the extent of risk-based pricing even when doing so would reduce overall market efficiency. Public attitudes toward risk-based pricing could also provide signals to legislators and regulators as to how they should weigh efficiency and equity in deciding on the degree to which they seek to constrain risk-based pricing. However, it should be acknowledged that consumers might not fully understand the trade-offs between risk-based pricing and risk sharing or might promote their own narrow self-interest, and it thus might be unwise for policymakers to blindly follow public sentiment.

---

[3] Adverse selection can, in principle, lead to a vicious circle in which continued efforts to subsidize high-risk policyholders can cause the market to shrink to the point that there is no longer an adequate pool of insured individuals over which to spread risk. However, insurance markets can still function in the presence of significant subsidies, even if the overall welfare generated by the market is less than it would be with risk-based rates (see Thomas Buchmueller and John DiNardo, "Did Community Rating Induce an Adverse Selection Death Spiral? Evidence from New York, Pennsylvania, and Connecticut," *American Economic Review*, Vol. 92, No. 1, March 2002). For an overview of the large and rapidly growing literature on the welfare analysis of insurance markets, see Liran Einav, Amy Finkelstein, and Neale Mahoney, "Chapter 14: The IO of Selection Markets," in Kate Ho, Ali Hortaçsu, and Alessandro Lizzer, eds., *Handbook of Industrial Organization*, Vol. 5, Elsevier, 2021. For an overview of the negative effects of restricting the use of adequate rating variables, see Lars Powell, "Risk-Based Pricing of Property and Liability Insurance," *Journal of Insurance Regulation*, Vol. 39, No. 4, 2020.

[4] Medical underwriting still exists in the individual and small group market in some states, but not for plans purchased through markets set up by the Affordable Care Act.

Despite the importance of understanding public attitudes toward risk-based pricing and risk-sharing, relatively little is known about collective attitudes toward risk-based pricing. Thus, we address the following research questions in this report:

- In what contexts does the public support insurance premiums that are based on individual risk factors?
- How much are people willing to pay to subsidize the premiums of higher-risk policyholders?
- How does support of pricing based on individual risk factors vary across demographic groups?

We base our answers to these questions on a survey of 867 individuals designed to be representative of the U.S. adult population. Our goal is to describe public attitudes toward risk-based pricing and inform legislative and regulatory policy discussions and decisions on insurance pricing. We do not aim to recommend what legislative and regulatory policy toward insurance pricing should be.

Prior Empirical Research

In a 2016 study, Heller and Styczynski examined public attitudes toward the use of different factors in setting auto insurance premiums. Based on a nationally representative survey of 1,000 Americans, they reported the percentage of the public that believed it is very fair, somewhat fair, somewhat unfair, or very unfair for insurers to use various factors in setting the auto insurance premium for a driver. The authors found high levels of support for the use of factors directly related to driving behavior: 84 percent believed it is very fair or somewhat fair to use moving violations, such as speeding tickets, in setting premiums, and 83 percent believed it is very or somewhat fair to use traffic accidents caused by the driver. In contrast, there was markedly less support for using nondriving factors in setting auto insurance premiums. Less than 30 percent found it very or somewhat fair to use credit scores, marital status, level of education, and several other nondriving factors to set rates.[5] The findings are relevant to questions addressed in our study because they provide insight into the circumstances in which people believe it is fair to set premiums based on factors associated with higher risk. A drawback of Heller and Styczynski's approach, however, is that survey respondents were given no information on whether the factors examined are actually correlated with expected insured loss.

In 2021, Kiviat conducted a nationally representative survey that asked respondents to indicate how fair it is for auto insurers and lenders to use different types of data to predict

---

[5] Douglas Heller and Michelle Styczynski, *Major Auto Insurers Raise Rates Based on Economic Factors: Low- and Moderate-Income Drivers Charged Higher Premiums*, Consumer Federation of America, June 27, 2016, p. 4.

consumer behavior and to set insurance premiums.[6] In the auto insurance setting, 16 types of data were considered, including credit scores, speeding tickets, income, gender, race, and grocery store purchases. Kiviat found that whether Americans think it is fair to use data for these purposes depends on the type of data and the context in which it is used. For example, the use of data on speeding tickets by auto insurers was viewed as very fair or somewhat fair by 75 percent of Americans. The use of data on race and ethnicity, in contrast, was viewed as very fair or somewhat fair by only 11 percent of Americans. She found that respondents felt that in some cases, data on behavioral markers, such as speeding tickets, were fair to use in setting insurance premiums, but that such data were not fair to use in all contexts. She also found that Americans were more supportive of using data that are logically related to the risk under consideration. We extend Kiviat's work by expanding the insurance lines considered and also by developing estimates of how much people believe it is appropriate for the premiums of lower-risk policyholders to be increased to reduce the premiums of higher-risk policyholders from risk-based prices.

Heller and Styczynski's and Kiviat's work provides a valuable benchmark for the findings in this study, and we compare our findings with the findings in these two studies in Chapter 3.

Terminology

Figure 1.1 illustrates the spectrum of pricing approaches examined in this study. At one end of the spectrum is risk-based pricing. *Risk-based pricing* reflects the full difference in risk across policyholder groups.[7] At the other end of the spectrum is full risk-sharing. We define *full risk-sharing* as situations in which all policyholders pay the same premium regardless of risk.[8] Lower-risk policyholders do not cross-subsidize higher-risk policyholders when pricing is risk-based, and cross-subsidies increase as one moves along the spectrum from risk-based pricing to full risk-sharing.

---

[6] Barbara Kiviat, "Which Data Fairly Differentiate? American Views on the Use of Personal Data in Two Market Settings," *Sociological Science*, Vol. 8, January 2021.

[7] This definition of *risk-based pricing* is consistent with that used by the Insurance Information Institute. According to the Insurance Information Institute, *risk-based pricing* means "offering different prices for the same level of coverage, based on risk factors specific to the insured person or property. If policies were not priced this way—if insurers had to come up with a one-size-fits-all price for auto coverage that didn't consider vehicle type and use, where and how much the car will be driven, and so forth—lower-risk drivers would subsidize riskier ones" (Insurance Information Institute, *Trends and Insights: Risk-Based Pricing of Insurance*, September 2022, p. 1). As discussed earlier, perfect risk-based pricing is not likely achievable in practice and represents a theoretical endpoint of the pricing spectrum.

[8] In health insurance settings, full risk-sharing is typically referred to as *community pricing* (see Buchmueller and DiNardo, 2002).

FIGURE 1.1

Spectrum of Pricing Approaches Considered in This Study

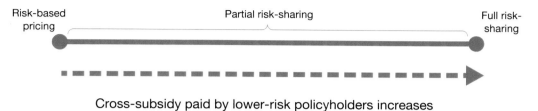

Cross-subsidy paid by lower-risk policyholders increases

We refer to points on the pricing spectrum between risk-based pricing and full risk-sharing as *partial risk-sharing*. We also distinguish between full risk-sharing and all other points on the pricing spectrum. *Pricing based on individual risk factors* refers to situations in which the premiums charged to higher-risk policyholders are greater than those charged to lower-risk policyholders, but the difference does not necessarily reflect the full difference in risk. Risk-based pricing is thus a special case of pricing based on individual risk factors.

In our exposition, we distinguish between risk factors and risk. *Risk factors* are observable characteristics of policyholders that predict higher-than-average insured losses. We reserve *risk* to describe the expected insured losses for the policyholder. We also distinguish cross-subsidies from government subsidies. *Cross-subsidies* are increases in premiums paid by lower-risk policyholders that lower the premiums for higher-risk policyholders. *Government subsidies* are paid to reduce the premiums for some or all policyholders by a government entity outside the market. *Subsidies* is a catchall for cross-subsidies or government subsidies.

Report Organization

In Chapter 2 we discuss the research methodology. We present the survey questions and discuss the considerations underlying their design. The survey sample and response rates are also described. In Chapter 3, we present findings for each of the research questions. In Chapter 4, we evaluate the findings and offer conclusions about their implications for insurance regulation, climate change, and behavioral economics. Three appendixes provide additional detail. The survey instrument is reproduced in Appendix A, and the demographic characteristics of the sample are provided in Appendix B. The statistical methods used in the analysis are described in Appendix C. In Appendix D, we provide additional analysis of survey responses on rate plans.

CHAPTER 2

Survey Methods

In this chapter, we first discuss the survey questions developed to assess attitudes toward risk-based pricing. We then describe the mechanism used to field the survey and the resulting dataset.

Survey Design

We developed two types of questions to assess attitudes toward insurance premiums based on individual risk factors. In the first set of questions, survey respondents are asked whether policyholders should pay more for insurance based on specific risk factors.[1] Examples of this type of question include the following:

- Assume that health care costs are higher for women. Do you think that women should pay more for health insurance?
- Assume that the chance of causing an accident is higher for drivers with more speeding tickets. Should drivers with more speeding tickets pay more for car insurance?
- Do you think a homeowner should pay more for flood insurance if the home is at higher risk of flooding than other homes?

The complete list of survey questions is provided in Appendix A.

In each case, we asked respondents to *assume* that the risk factor in question is associated with higher losses. We did so to focus the respondent on the fairness of charging more for the risk rather than speculating about the actual relationship between the risk factor in question and the underlying risk.[2]

---

[1] See Questions 1_1, 1_2, 1_3, and 1_4 in Appendix A.

[2] The posited relationships between the risk factors and costs are plausible, but we are not asserting that the factors are actually associated with costs in the manner specified.

To assess the extent to which attitudes toward pricing based on individual risk factors vary in different settings, we constructed questions relevant to each of the following types of insurance:

- health insurance
- term life insurance
- auto insurance
- flood insurance.

The types of loss covered by insurance in each of these settings obviously differ. For health insurance, at issue is the cost of health care treatment. For term life insurance, monetary payments are made to designated beneficiaries if the policyholder dies during the policy period (the policy term). Auto insurance provides liability coverage for bodily injury or property damage claims brought by third parties and can cover damage to the policyholder's vehicle (first-party coverage). Flood insurance covers damage to the structure owned by the policyholder and can cover the contents for owners or renters.

The individual risk factors we selected for examination vary by the extent to which individuals are able to control the characteristic in question. This allowed us to examine the extent to which attitudes toward pricing based on individual risk factors vary along this dimension.

We also included risk factors at issue in policy discussions and debates over risk-based pricing. In the auto insurance setting, for example, we asked whether individuals with lower credit scores should pay more for auto insurance, an important topic in light of the prevalent use of this factor among auto insurers.[3] In the flood insurance setting, we asked whether homeowners should pay more for flood insurance if the increase in premiums were due to sea level rise. When flood risk maps are updated, the National Flood Insurance Program (NFIP) has allowed premiums to be based on the previous map (so-called grandfathering), and current NFIP efforts to move to risk-based rates would eliminate this practice. Motivated by these changes, we asked whether homeowners should pay more if their flood risk has increased due to sea level rise.

This first type of question provides information on whether the public supports pricing based on individual risk factors in particular situations, but it does not provide information on the degree to which premiums should reflect the underlying risk. In addition, survey respondents might not consider who would pay any subsidy. For example, respondents might assume that the federal or state government would pay the subsidy. The second type of survey question addresses these limitations. To do this, we presented survey respondents with three or four different rate plans and asked respondents to rank the plans in order of preference.[4] At one extreme, all policyholders pay the same premium regardless of their individual risk. At

---

[3] States that allow and do not allow credit scoring in pricing auto insurance are listed in Susan Meyer, "Car Insurance Rating Factors by State," The Zebra, webpage, undated.

[4] See Questions 2_1, 2_2, 2_3, and 2_4 in Appendix A.

the other, premiums are risk-based—that is, they reflect the risk posed by the individual policyholder. In the second type of questions, low-risk policyholders usually pay any subsidies (low-risk policyholders cross-subsidize high-risk policyholders), although survey respondents are not explicitly alerted to this fact.

Table 2.1 describes the rate plans offered in a health insurance setting. Survey respondents are told that the expected annual health care costs are $30,000 for people with leukemia and $10,000 for healthy people of the same age. In Rate Plan A, the health insurance premium for John, who has leukemia, is $30,000 a year, and the health insurance premium for healthy people John's age is $10,000. In this risk-based pricing scheme, healthy people pay no subsidy for John's premium, and John receives no premium subsidy. At the other extreme, people with and without leukemia pay the same premium (Rate Plan B—full risk-sharing). As shown in the last column of Table 2.1, all policyholders pay $12,000 for coverage. Healthy people pay $2,000 each to subsidize the premiums of those with leukemia, and people with leukemia each receive an $18,000 premium subsidy. The premiums and implied subsidies in this rating plan are calculated based on an assumption that 10 percent of the population has leukemia and are subject to the requirement that the total amount of premium across all policyholders is equal to the total expected health care costs—that is, that the rating plan overall is actuarially sound. Rate Plan C provides a middle ground in which the higher risk of people with leukemia is partially shared with healthy policyholders.

Designing the second type of survey question in this way has several advantages. First, by imposing the condition that each of the overall plans is actuarially sound, it implicitly requires respondents to acknowledge that someone has to pay the costs of the subsidy and the magnitude of the payments. Second, it requires survey respondents to consider who is going

TABLE 2.1
Rate Plan Options in the Health Insurance Scenario

Rate Plan Characteristic	Rate Plan A (Risk-Based Pricing)	Rate Plan C (Partial Risk-Sharing)	Rate Plan B (Full Risk-Sharing)
Healthy people John's age (individuals paying subsidy)			
Premium per person	$10,000	$11,000	$12,000
Subsidy paid per person	0	$1,000	$2,000
Percentage change in premium per person	0	10	20
People with leukemia John's age (individuals receiving subsidy)			
Premium per person	$30,000	$20,000	$12,000
Subsidy received per person	0	$10,000	$18,000
Percentage change in premium per person	0	−33	−60

SOURCE: Authors' analysis of the survey protocol.

NOTE: Assumes that 90 percent of the population John's age are healthy and that 10 percent have the condition.

to pay the subsidy. Survey respondents are not explicitly told that lower-risk policyholders pay the subsidy, but that assumption is embedded in the scenarios.

A second rating plan scenario was developed in the health insurance setting, in which the increased risk was due to heavy drinking instead of leukemia. This scenario allows us to examine support for the same subsidy levels in a context where the increased risk is more under the control of the individual.

Two flood insurance rating scenarios were also developed. In the first, the risk-based premiums are $500 and $2,500 for homes in low-risk and high-risk flood areas, respectively. One-half of the homes are assumed to be in each area, and respondents choose between plans with risk-based pricing, partial risk-sharing, and full risk-sharing (Table 2.2). The subsidies paid by low-risk policyholders are similar in magnitude to those in the health insurance scenarios. However, the percentage increases in the premiums of low-risk policyholders due to the subsidies are much larger.

TABLE 2.2

Rate Plan Options in the Flood Insurance Scenario

Rate Plan Characteristic	Rate Plan A (Risk-Based Pricing)	Rate Plan C (Partial Risk-Sharing)	Rate Plan B (Full Risk-Sharing)
Homes in low-risk areas (homeowners paying subsidy)			
Premium per home	$500	$1,000	$1,500
Subsidy paid per home	0	$500	$1,000
Percentage change in premium per home	0	100	200
Homes in high-risk areas (homeowners receiving subsidy)			
Premium per home	$2,500	$2,000	$1,500
Subsidy received per home	0	$500	$1,000
Percentage change in premium per home	0	−20	−40

SOURCE: Authors' analysis of the survey protocol.

NOTE: Assumes that 50 percent of homes are in areas with high flood risk and 50 percent are in areas with low flood risk.

A second flood insurance scenario posits that the risk-based prices have been adopted and that over a ten-year period, the risk of homes in the high-risk areas has further increased due to sea level rise. Respondents are asked to rank rate plans similar to those in the first flood insurance scenario but this time are also offered a plan in which the federal government pays the increase in premium due to sea level rise (Table 2.3). The scenario provides insight into preferences when the change is due to phenomena beyond the control of homeowners in high-risk areas. It also provides insight into the potential opposition that the Federal Emergency Management Agency (FEMA) might encounter as it moves to risk-based pricing for flood insurance and the extent of public support for federal flood insurance affordability programs that provide assistance to pay flood insurance premiums.

TABLE 2.3

Rate Plan Options in the Flood Insurance Scenario with Government Subsidy Program

Rate Plan Characteristic	Rate Plan D (Risk-Based Pricing)	Rate Plan F (Partial Risk-Sharing)	Rate Plan E (Full Risk-Sharing)	Rate Plan G (Government Subsidy)
Homes in low-risk areas (homeowners paying subsidy)				
Premium per home	$500	$1,000	$2,000	$500
Subsidy paid per home	0	$500	$1,500	0
Percentage change in premium per home	0	100	300	0
Homes in high-risk areas (homeowners receiving subsidy)				
Premium per home	$3,500	$3,000	$2,000	$2,500
Subsidy received per home	0	$500	$1,500	$1,000
Percentage change in premium per home	0	−14	−43	−29
Subsidy paid by federal taxpayers				
Subsidy paid per home	0	0	0	$1,000

SOURCE: Authors' analysis of the survey protocol.

NOTE: Assumes that 50 percent of homes are in areas with high flood risk and 50 percent are in areas with low flood risk.

Survey Fielding

We administered a web-based survey using RAND's American Life Panel (ALP). The RAND ALP is a nationally representative, probability-based panel of approximately 6,000 individuals. The standing nature of the panel ensures that response rates are high, attrition is minimized, and responses are high-quality.[5] Respondents are asked to complete 6–12 surveys over the course of a year and receive $20 in compensation for surveys estimated to take 30 minutes (prorated for shorter surveys). If needed, respondents are provided with a computer and internet access to ensure representativeness of the panel.

In mid-December 2021, 1,216 individuals were invited to participate in the survey. By the time the survey closed in late January 2022, 867 individuals had completed the survey (71.3 percent). Respondents answered all the questions for the first type of question.[6] Completion rates were also high for the second type of question—between 88 and 92 percent of survey participants fully ranked the rating plans, depending on the scenario, and 99 percent of survey participants fully or partially ranked the rating plans.[7] The ALP provided weights with the survey responses that match the set of respondents to the adult U.S. population, as characterized by the U.S. Census Bureau and U.S. Bureau of Labor Statistics' Current Population Survey, and we used these weights in our analysis. The demographic characteristics of the sample, both unweighted and weighted, are provided in Appendix B.

---

[5] See Michael Pollard and Matthew D. Baird, *The RAND American Life Panel: Technical Description*, RAND Corporation, RR-1651, 2017; RAND Corporation, "About the American Life Panel," webpage, undated.

[6] Survey Questions 1_1, 1_2, 1_3, and 1_4 in Appendix A.

[7] See Table D.1 in Appendix D.

CHAPTER 3

Findings

In this chapter, we present findings for the three research questions posed in Chapter 1. We first examine the proportion of the U.S. adult population that supports higher premiums for individuals with specific risk factors. We then explore *how much* respondents believe low-risk policyholders should pay to subsidize the premiums of high-risk policyholders. Finally, we examine the relationship between demographic characteristics and support for pricing based on individual risk factors.

Is There Support for Pricing Based on Individual Risk Factors?

We examine support for pricing based on individual risk factors in four different insurance settings: health, term life, auto, and flood. Findings for each are presented in turn.

Health Insurance

Figure 3.1 presents the findings on attitudes toward basing health insurance premiums on individual risk factors in a health insurance setting. As detailed in Chapter 2, survey respondents were directed to assume that the risk factor in question is indeed associated with higher health care costs when considering how to respond. The green portion of the bar indicates the estimated percentage of the U.S. adult population who support or strongly support higher premiums for individuals in the indicated group. What is not known is how much higher the respondents making their selections think the premium should be. It could be slightly more than the rates paid by other policyholders or sufficiently higher to equal the risk-based price for this subgroup. The red portion of the bars show the percentage of the population who oppose or strongly oppose higher premiums for the indicated group. Respondents making these selections thus support equal premiums for people with or without the risk factor in question, other things being equal.[1]

---

[1] The margin of error of the estimates (based on a 95-percent statistical confidence interval) ranges from plus or minus 2 percentage points to plus or minus 5 percentage points depending on the risk factor (see Table C.1 in Appendix C).

FIGURE 3.1

Public Support for Higher Health Insurance Premiums by Risk Factor

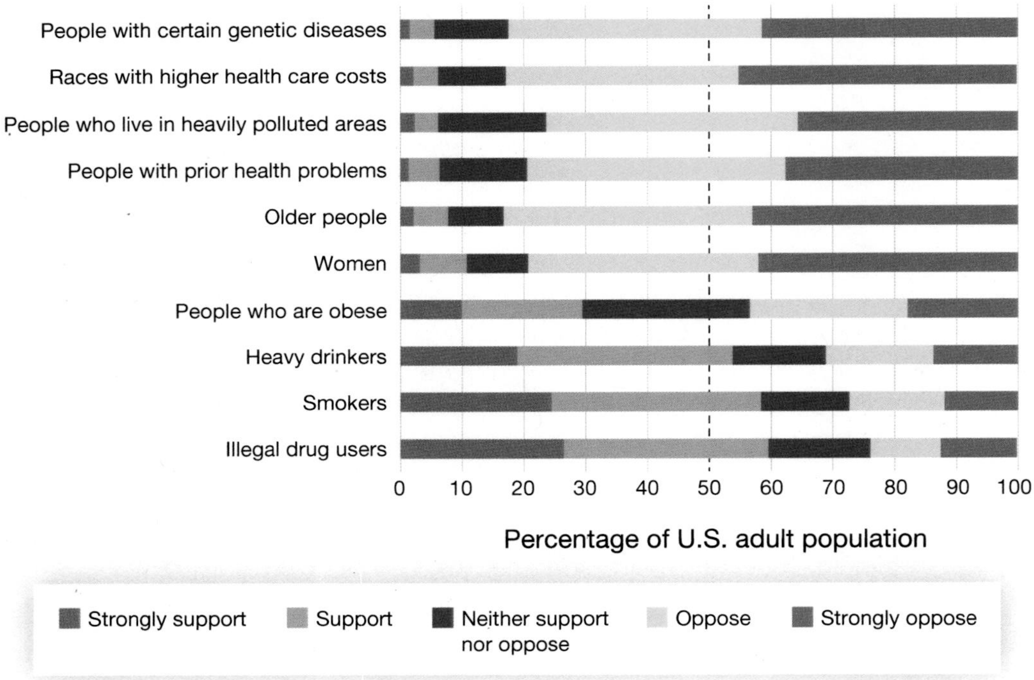

Percentage of U.S. adult population

- Strongly support
- Support
- Neither support nor oppose
- Oppose
- Strongly oppose

SOURCE: Authors' analysis of survey responses.

Only a small percentage of the U.S. adult population support the position that people with certain genetic diseases should pay more for health insurance. As shown by the green portion of the top bar in Figure 3.1, approximately 6 percent of the population support or strongly support the position that people with genetic diseases should pay more for health insurance. This low level of support implies little support for pricing based on this risk factor. As shown by the red portion of the bars, approximately 80 percent of the population support equal premiums for people with and without certain genetic diseases. Similarly, there are low levels of support for charging more based on race; whether the individual lives in a polluted area; and prior health problems, such as asthma, diabetes, or cancer.[2]

There is slightly more support, but still less than 10 percent, for charging older people more for health insurance than younger people. Charging more based on costs associated with gender received just more than 10 percent support.

---

[2] Race is a prohibited rating factor in every state.

In contrast, more than one-half of the U.S. adult population support charging more for policyholders who drink heavily, smoke, or use illegal drugs. These behaviors are thought to be more under one's control and have traditionally been considered vices.[3] Even though a referendum that supports higher insurance premiums for these groups might pass, a substantial minority of the population do not believe that these groups should be charged more for health insurance. And even though a majority of the population believe that these groups should pay more, we do not know how much more—it could be that many believe that the premiums should still be below the risk-based rate. We will return to this issue later in this chapter.

At approximately 30 percent, the percentage of the population who support higher rates for people who are obese is higher than those for risk factors that are perceived as outside one's control (such as gender or genetic conditions) but less than rates for risk factors that are thought to be more under one's control. This result perhaps reflects widely divergent views regarding the extent to which individuals can effectively control their weight through behavioral changes.

Term Life Insurance

The findings for term life insurance were very similar to those for health insurance, although there appears to be somewhat more support for pricing based on individual risk factors for term life insurance. Figure 3.2 compares the percentage of the population either supporting or strongly supporting higher premiums by risk factor for health insurance and term life insurance. As can be seen, the percentages supporting higher premiums for illegal drug use, smoking, and heavy drinking are similar. In contrast, there is greater support for higher term life premiums for risk factors outside one's control than for health insurance. Even though the percentage of the population supporting higher premiums for these subgroups is higher for term life, it remains low. For example, the percentage supporting or strongly supporting higher term life premiums for older adults is still only slightly above 20 percent. We have no data on the reasons for these differences, but a belief by many respondents that, in contrast to term life insurance, health insurance is a necessity is a possible explanation.

---

[3] Kiviat, 2021, p. 31. Kiviat considers such individual characteristics as these to be "behavioral" (p. 35). She notes that the "ostensibly deliberate" (p. 35) actions that underlie these behaviors contrast with the lack of such actions for "nonbehavioral" characteristics, such as age or gender.

FIGURE 3.2

Public Support for Higher Term Life Insurance Premiums by Risk Factor

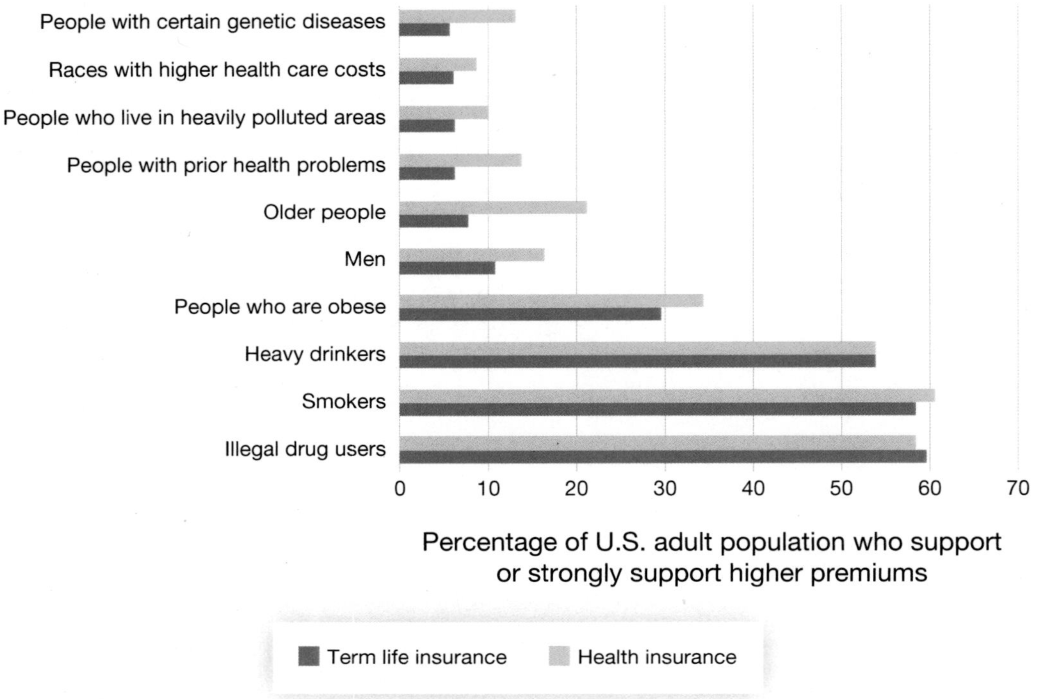

Percentage of U.S. adult population who support
or strongly support higher premiums

Term life insurance   Health insurance

SOURCE: Authors' analysis of survey responses.

Auto Insurance

As with health and term life insurance, the percentage of the U.S. adult population who believe that individual risk factors should affect auto insurance premiums varies a great deal across the risk factors considered. When asked to assume that the chance of causing an accident increases with more speeding tickets, more than 80 percent support or strongly support higher premiums for this group.[4] Almost 60 percent support higher insurance prices for younger drivers, and about 45 percent support higher premiums for drivers of faster cars (Figure 3.3).

In contrast, there is little popular support for basing premiums on the other risk factors considered. Less than 10 percent of respondents believe that race or credit scores are appropriate factors for pricing when directed to assume that the chance of causing an accident is

---

[4] The severity of auto accidents may also be higher for drivers with more speeding tickets, but we only mentioned frequency in the question. Perhaps a higher proportion of the population would support higher rates for drivers with more speeding tickets if respondents were directed to assume that both accident frequency and severity increased.

FIGURE 3.3

Public Support for Higher Auto Insurance Premiums by Risk Factor

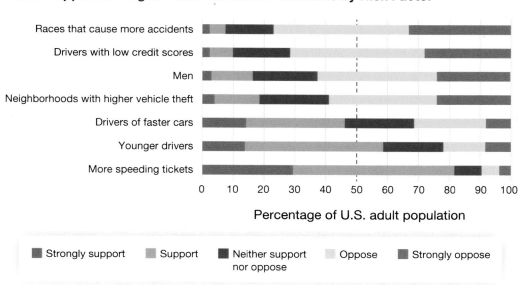

SOURCE: Authors' analysis of survey responses.

higher for people of certain races or for drivers with low credit scores.[5] Less than 20 percent support using gender as a factor for pricing when told to assume that the chance of causing an accident is higher for men. When directed to assume that the chance of a vehicle being stolen is higher in certain neighborhoods, less than 20 percent support or strongly support higher premiums for drivers who live in those neighborhoods.

Three observations about these findings merit discussion. First, these findings are broadly consistent with prior empirical work discussed in Chapter 1. Recall from Chapter 1 that Kiviat asked survey respondents to rate the fairness of using various sorts of personal data to predict who would file insurance claims and to charge those people higher premiums for car insurance or to decline to offer them coverage altogether. Heller and Styczynski reported the percentage of the public that believed it very fair, somewhat fair, somewhat unfair, or very unfair for insurers to use various factors in setting auto insurance premiums. Our results are similar for three of the five risk factors for which comparisons could be made (see top three rows of Table 3.1). An area of less agreement is neighborhood, although the difference could be due, in part, to how the question was phrased—Kiviat asked if zip code should be used to

---

[5] Respondents were asked whether drivers with low credit scores should pay more for car insurance, but the type of credit score was not described. Specifically, respondents were not asked about credit-based insurance scores (CBISs), the type of credit scores now being used by some insurers. Credit scores predict credit delinquency, whereas CBISs predict insurance losses. Nevertheless, both are based on a person's credit report (Insurance Information Institute, undated). If CBISs were used in the question and the meaning defined, support for credit scores could conceivably be higher than that observed in this survey.

predict who would file claims, whereas we used the less precisely defined concept of neighborhood. The largest discrepancy was found for credit score. Kiviat found that 36 percent indicated that it is fair or very fair to use credit scores to predict who would file claims and set auto rates, compared with our finding that 10 percent (see Figure 3.3) support or strongly support charging higher premiums for drivers with low credit scores. Heller and Styczynski found 38 percent. The differences perhaps reflect change in attitudes toward credit scores. It should be noted, however, that considerably less than one-half of the population in all three studies support basing auto premiums on credit scores.

Second, our findings for auto insurance do not line up neatly with expectations of higher support for pricing based on individual risk factors for behaviors more under an individual's control. For example, more than 50 percent of the population support or strongly support higher car insurance premiums for younger drivers—a risk factor beyond the control of the driver.[6] The findings for credit scores show the converse, with only 10 percent supporting rates based on a behavior that the driver can ostensibly control. These results suggest that the assessment of when it is appropriate to base insurance premiums on individual attributes is more nuanced than simply determining whether the behavior or risk factor is under one's control. For example, credit scores may not be perceived to be sufficiently relevant to driving behavior, even if it turns out that low credit scores are correlated with higher accident rates.[7]

TABLE 3.1

Consistency of Auto Insurance Findings with Those in Previous Studies (Percentage of Americans Supporting Use of Factor in Setting Premiums)

Factor	This Study[a]		Estimate from Kiviat[b]	Estimate from Heller and Styczynski[c]
	Estimate	95-Percent Confidence Interval		
Race	8	[5, 10]	11	N/A
Gender	16	[13, 20]	16	N/A
Speeding tickets	82	[77, 85]	75	84
Neighborhood where driver lives	19	[15, 22]	31	N/A
Credit score	10	[7, 13]	36	38

SOURCE: Authors' analysis of survey responses and review of studies by Kiviat, 2021, and Heller and Styczynski, 2016.

NOTE: N/A = not applicable because these factors were not examined.

[a] Percentage of U.S. adult population who support or strongly support higher premiums for the group under the assumption that the chance of causing an accident is associated with this factor.

[b] Percentage of Americans who believe it is somewhat fair or very fair to use data on the factor to predict consumer behavior and set insurance premiums.

[c] Percentage of Americans who believe it is somewhat fair or very fair to use the factor to set auto insurance premiums.

---

[6] Youths may be able to choose not to drive at all and thus have partial control over the risk.

[7] Kiviat (2021, p. 37) finds that survey respondents consider "logical relatedness" in evaluating whether it is fair for lenders or insurers to use data to predict risk and to set lending rates or insurance premiums.

Finally, there is also considerable disjuncture between our findings and the factors that state regulators allow insurers to use in setting premiums. The low percentage of the population who support or strongly support higher premiums for drivers who live in neighborhoods with higher vehicle theft contrasts with the fact that all states allow insurers to use zip code or address in setting premiums.[8] Similarly, only a handful of states prohibit credit score or gender from being used in setting premiums, which is at odds with the low public support for basing premiums on these factors.[9]

Flood Insurance

We found solid support for premiums that vary based on flood risk in some, but not all, situations (see Figure 3.4). Approximately two-thirds of the U.S. adult population support higher premiums for homes that are at higher risk of flooding (last row of Table 3.4). However, about 20 percent of the population oppose or strongly oppose such price variation, implying that they believe that flood risk should be spread evenly across all homeowners. And even though two-thirds support higher premiums, some might favor something short of risk-based pricing. Responses were similar for homes at which there has been prior flood damage that suggests greater risk of future flooding. The percentage of the population supporting or strongly supporting higher premiums in this case dropped to 60 percent. This decline perhaps reflects survey language indicating that the prior damage only *suggests* that the property is at greater risk of future flooding (see Question 1_1 in Appendix A): Properties with prior damage may not be at greater risk of future loss if flood risk has been mitigated (such as by elevating the structure) or if past losses were due to chance (or more informally, "bad luck") that does not reflect the long-term risk at the property.

Although a solid majority of the population support the general concept that flood insurance premiums should be higher for homes at higher flood risk, support falls to less than 50 percent when the particular details of the situation are considered. If the home is at higher risk but the homeowner has limited assets and low income, the percentage of the population supporting or strongly supporting higher premiums drops to less than 40 percent. If the higher risk is due to factors that are beyond the homeowner's control, support for higher premiums declines further. Specifically, if the homeowner has lived in the home for many years, but flood risk has recently increased due to sea level rise, then the proportion of the population supporting or strongly supporting higher premiums declines to approximately one-third. If the insured had been in the home for a long time, and the risk recently increased due to nearby property development, support for higher premiums drops to just more than 20 percent.

---

[8] Although we asked respondents about neighborhoods, we did not ask any questions about attitudes toward basing pricing on region or population density. For example, charging rural residents lower rates than urbanites might be more acceptable than pricing by neighborhood. This question could be explored in future research.

[9] For rating factors allowed by state, see Meyer, undated.

FIGURE 3.4

Public Support for Higher Flood Insurance Premiums by Risk Factor

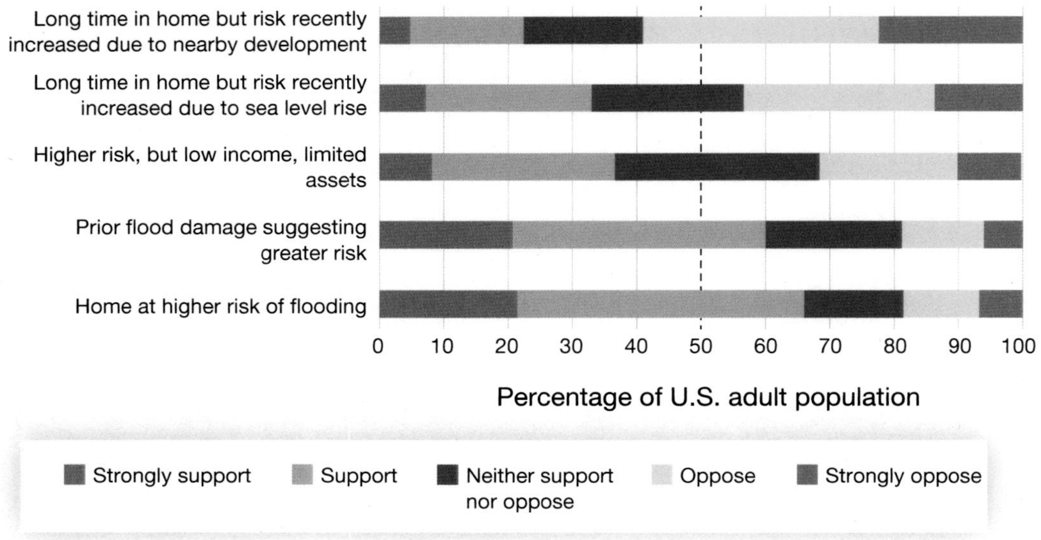

Percentage of U.S. adult population

Strongly support   Support   Neither support   Oppose   Strongly oppose
nor oppose

SOURCE: Authors' analysis of survey responses.

How Much Are People Willing to Pay on Subsidies?

In the previous section, we examined the circumstances under which survey respondents thought it appropriate for policyholders to pay more if they pose higher risk. If such policyholders do not pay more, the insurance premiums are subsidized by either lower-risk policyholders or some other source. The survey questions in the previous section did not discuss who was going to pay the subsidy or how much it would be. In this section, we quantify how much people would be willing to subsidize high-risk policyholders—first in a health insurance setting and then in a flood insurance setting. As detailed in Chapter 2, these estimates are based on the responses to survey questions in which respondents are asked to rank three or four insurance rate plans that vary in how much lower-risk policyholders subsidize higher-risk policyholders. The plans under consideration are all actuarially sound in that the total amount collected from all policyholders equals the expected aggregate claim payments. Survey respondents thus must consider the burden on those who must fund the subsidy in formulating their responses. An enumeration of survey responses and their internal consistency is provided in Appendix D.

Health Insurance

In the first health insurance scenario, the health insurance premiums of the small percentage of the population with leukemia are subsidized by healthy individuals to varying degrees. At one extreme, premiums are based on risk, and there are no subsidies: Those with leukemia pay $30,000 per year, and those without leukemia pay $10,000. At the other extreme, health care costs are spread across the population, and all policyholders pay $12,000 per year. An intermediate plan, in which risks are partially shared, is also offered (see Chapter 2 for details).

A substantial majority of the population prefer the rate plan in which the low-risk individuals pay a considerable subsidy. As shown in the bottom row of Table 3.2, nearly two-thirds of the U.S. adult population prefer the rate plan in which low-risk policyholders each pay an additional $2,000 per year to subsidize the premiums of people with leukemia, increasing the premium paid by low-risk policyholders by 20 percent. Another 24 percent prefer the plan in which low-risk policyholders pay $1,000 to subsidize the premiums of policyholders with leukemia. Only 10 percent of the population prefer the risk-based rate plan.[10]

More detailed analysis of how respondents ranked the three rating plans allows further insight into the preferred subsidy levels. Under reasonable assumptions about the social welfare functions that respondents used to rank the rating plans, we can infer that at least 57 percent of the U.S. adult population prefer a subsidy that increases the premium of low-risk

TABLE 3.2

Preferred Subsidy Levels in a Health Insurance Setting: Leukemia Scenario

Rate Plan	Low-Risk Policyholders		High-Risk Policyholders		Percentage of Population Preferring Plan[b]	95-Percent Confidence Interval
	Subsidy Paid ($/policyholder per year)	Percentage Change in Premium[a]	Subsidy Received ($/policyholder per year)	Percentage Change in Premium[a]		
Risk-based pricing	0	0	0	0	10	[8, 13]
Partial risk-sharing	1,000	10	10,000	−33	24	[19, 30]
Full risk-sharing	2,000	20	18,000	−60	66	[60, 71]

SOURCE: Authors' analysis of survey responses.

[a] Risk-based premium per year is $10,000 for healthy people and $30,000 for people with leukemia.

[b] Based on 856 respondents who indicated a first choice.

---

[10] It is interesting to note that support for full risk-sharing is less than indicated by responses to the survey questions asked to gauge qualitative support for individual risk-based premiums. Responses to the questions regarding people with certain genetic conditions and people with prior health problems are most analogous to those analyzed in the leukemia scenario here. Recall from Figure 3.1 that 82 percent of the population oppose higher premiums for people with certain genetic diseases and 80 percent oppose higher premiums for those with prior health problems. Thus, 80–82 percent support full risk-sharing. This level of support is considerably higher than the 66 percent who preferred the rating plan with full risk-sharing—and there are undoubtedly some respondents who prefer a high level of risk-sharing, but not full risk-sharing. The findings suggest that the initial impulse to help a socially sympathetic group is tempered when survey respondents more concretely consider the costs involved. We did not detect such an effect in the heavy-drinking and flood insurance scenarios subsequently discussed in this chapter (although we cannot rule out that an effect of more modest size exists).

policyholders by $1,000 and $2,000 per year. The percentage could be considerably higher, although the lack of variation in the partial risk-sharing scenario presented to survey respondents does not allow useful estimates (see Appendix D).

Public support for subsidies is considerably lower when it is the health care premiums of people who drink heavily that are being subsidized. In this scenario, somewhat less than one-half of the population (44 percent) prefer the plan with no subsidies (see Table 3.3). However, there is still considerable support for substantial subsidies for people who drink heavily, even though the subsidies might not rise to the levels required to charge equal premiums to people who do and do not drink heavily. Summing the estimates in the last two rows of Table 3.3 indicates that 56 percent of the population prefer rate plans in which people who do not drink heavily pay premiums that are 10 or 20 percent higher to subsize the premiums of people who drink heavily.

In this case, we can infer that at least 31 percent of the U.S. adult population prefer a subsidy that increases the premium of people who do not drink heavily by $1,000 and $2,000 per year. The percentage could be considerably higher, although the lack of variation in the partial risk-sharing scenario presented to survey respondents does not allow useful estimates (see Appendix D).

TABLE 3.3

Preferred Subsidy Levels in a Health Insurance Setting: Heavy-Drinking Scenario

Rate Plan	Low-Risk Policyholders		High-Risk Policyholders		Percentage of Population Preferring Plan[b]	95-Percent Confidence Interval
	Subsidy Paid ($/policyholder per year)	Percentage Change in Premium[a]	Subsidy Received ($/policyholder per year)	Percentage Change in Premium[a]		
Risk-based pricing	0	0	0	0	44	[38, 49]
Partial risk-sharing	1,000	10	10,000	−33	20	[16, 25]
Full risk-sharing	2,000	20	18,000	−60	36	[31, 42]

SOURCE: Authors' analysis of survey responses.

[a] Risk-based premium per year is $10,000 for nonheavy drinkers and $30,000 for heavy drinkers.

[b] Based on 858 respondents who indicated a first choice.

Flood Insurance

The results for the first flood insurance scenario we examined are similar to those for the heavy-drinking scenario. In this scenario, survey respondents are asked to consider different rating plans for homes in areas of high and low risk of flooding. The subsidies paid by owners of low-risk homes in each plan are similar in magnitude to those in the health insurance examples (see first column of Table 3.4), although considerably higher when expressed as a percentage of the risk-based premium on low-risk homes. Just more than 30 percent of the population prefer the rate plan in which owners of low-risk homes pay $1,000 in subsidy (last row of Table 3.4). This level of support is similar to the 36 percent who support the shared-risk plan in the heavy-drinking scenario. As in the heavy-drinking scenario, risk-based pricing is the most preferred rating plan, gaining support from somewhat less than one-half of the population. That said, it remains the case that more than one-half of the population (24 percent plus 31 percent) prefer pricing plans in which homeowners in low-risk areas pay 100 and 200 percent more than would be the case if premiums were risk-based.

In this flood insurance scenario, we can infer that at least 24 percent of the U.S. adult population prefer a subsidy that increases the premium of low-risk policyholders by $500 and $1,000 per year. The percentage could be considerably higher, although the lack of variation in the partial risk-sharing scenario presented to survey respondents does not allow useful estimates (see Appendix D).

TABLE 3.4

Preferred Subsidy Levels in a Flood Insurance Setting

Rate Plan	Low-Risk Policyholders		High-Risk Policyholders		Percentage of Population Preferring Plan[b]	95-Percent Confidence Interval
	Subsidy Paid ($/policyholder per year)	Percentage Change in Premium[a]	Subsidy Received ($/policyholder per year)	Percentage Change in Premium[a]		
Risk-based pricing	0	0	0	0	45	[40, 51]
Partial risk-sharing	500	100	500	−20	24	[19, 30]
Full risk-sharing	1,000	200	1,000	−40	31	[26, 36]

SOURCE: Authors' analysis of survey responses.

[a] Risk-based premium per year is $500 for homes in low-risk areas and $2,500 for homes in high-risk areas.

[b] Based on 860 respondents who indicated a first choice.

The second flood insurance scenario starts with a base case in which homeowners in high- and low-risk areas are paying risk-based premiums, but then sea level rise causes the risk-based premiums in the low-risk areas to increase. Survey respondents were asked to rank different pricing plans, one of which includes federal taxpayers paying the increase in high-risk areas. At 31 percent, not a large proportion of the U.S. adult population prefer using federal tax revenue to cover the increase in risk to the other rate plans (see Table 3.5). The majority responded that the increase in risk should be borne by the pool of insured individuals in the community, with a relative preference for the three other rating plans similar to that when there was no option for a federal subsidy.

TABLE 3.5

Preferred Subsidy Levels in a Flood Insurance Setting with a Federal Subsidy

Rate Plan	Low-Risk Policyholders		High-Risk Policyholders		Percentage of Population Preferring Plan[b]	95-Percent Confidence Interval
	Subsidy Paid ($/policyholder per year)	Percentage Change in Premium[a]	Subsidy Received ($/policyholder per year)	Percentage Change in Premium[a]		
Risk-based pricing	0	0	0	0	31	[26, 37]
Partial risk-sharing	500	100	500	−14	15	[12, 18]
Full risk-sharing	1,500	300	1,500	−43	23	[19, 27]
Federal subsidy	0	0	1,000	−29	31	[26, 36]

SOURCE: Authors' analysis of survey responses.

[a] Risk-based premium per year is $500 for homes in low-risk areas and $3,500 for homes in high-risk areas.

[b] Based on 862 respondents who indicated a first choice.

Which Demographic Groups Are More Likely to Support Pricing Based on Risk Factors?

Our analysis so far has focused on attitudes toward risk-based pricing and cross-subsidization for the U.S. adult population as a whole. In this section, we examine whether and the extent to which these attitudes vary by demographic group. To do this, we use responses to the questions asking whether respondents support higher premiums for people with different risk factors. The ALP maintains and updates the demographic characteristics of the individuals participating on the panel, and we used these in our analysis. The statistical approach is described in Appendix C. The responses are analyzed separately for the four different insurance lines considered (health, term life, auto, and flood).

Table 3.6 reports the predictive margins for each of the demographic characteristics considered. The predictive margin shows the predicted probability of supporting or strongly supporting pricing based on risk factors, and the difference in the probabilities shows the effect of changing one demographic characteristic while holding the others constant.[11] The statistical significance of the difference relative to a reference category is indicated with green shading to denote greater support for pricing based on risk factors and orange shading to denote less support relative to the reference category. To examine whether the results for health insurance vary by the extent to which the risk factors are under an individual's control, we separated health risk factors that are more under an individual's control (illegal drug use, smoking, heavy drinking, and obesity) from the other risk factors.[12] Results for term life insurance are not reported because they are very similar to those for health insurance.

As shown in the second row of Table 3.6, men are more likely to support or strongly support pricing based on risk factors than women in all the lines examined, holding the other demographic factors constant. For example, men are 11 percentage points more likely to support or strongly support higher health insurance premiums for risk factors that are less under an individual's control than women (16 percent versus 5 percent), although in both cases, the percentage supporting higher premiums is low. The same difference is observed for health risk factors that are less under an individual's control. The percentage supporting or strongly supporting higher premiums for the auto risk factors and flood risk factors included in the survey for each of the lines is 10 percentage points higher for men than women. These differences reflect the average over the risk factors considered in each of these lines and could be higher or lower for individual risk factors.

---

[11] For example, the predicted margin for men is the probability that men support pricing based on risk factors when the gender indicator for each observation in the dataset is set to men and the other characteristics for each survey respondent are left at their reported values. The predictive margin in this case is close to, but not the same as, the observed percentage of men who support pricing based on risk factors. It provides a good sense of how the differences across groups compare to the overall level of support for pricing based on risk factors.

[12] The categorization is based on the judgment of the authors and includes the risk factors for which there was the greatest support for pricing based on risk factors (see Table 3.1). It does not necessarily reflect the views of survey respondents.

TABLE 3.6

Variation in Support for Pricing Based on Risk Factors by Demographic Characteristic (Predictive Margin, Percentage of Group Supporting)

Characteristic	Health Insurance		Auto Insurance (All Risk Factors)[c]	Flood Insurance (All Risk Factors)[d]
	Risk Factors Less Under Individual Control[a]	Risk Factors More Under Individual Control[b]		
Gender				
Female (reference)	5	50	33	43
Male	16***	61***	43***	53***
Family income				
<$35,000 (reference)	11	43	32	40
≥$35,000 and <$60,000	9	54**	37**	45
≥$60,000 and <$100,000	7	55*	38**	48**
≥$100,000	10	64***	42***	54***
Age				
18–44 (reference)	9	49	35	40
45–64	10	54	36	48***
≥65	9	62***	42***	54***
Race				
White (reference)	10	55	39	49
Black	6	42***	30***	40**
American Indian/ Alaska Native	16	69	41	48
Asian or Pacific Islander	13	59	33	38
Other	8	56	34*	44
Ethnicity				
Not Hispanic (reference)	9	54	38	47
Hispanic	9	58	36	46
Urban/rural location				
Rural (reference)	10	56	37	48
Urban	9	54	38	47

Table 3.6—Continued

| | Health Insurance | | | |
Characteristic	Risk Factors Less Under Individual Control[a]	Risk Factors More Under Individual Control[b]	Auto Insurance (All Risk Factors)[c]	Flood Insurance (All Risk Factors)[d]
Region of current residence				
New England and Middle Atlantic (reference)	7	53	37	45
South Atlantic	9	62**	35	51
North Central	10	55	39	51*
South Central	8	50	36	43
Mountain	12	57	41	47
Pacific	10	50	40	46

SOURCE: Authors' analysis of survey responses.

NOTE: The predictive margin shows the predicted probability of supporting or strongly supporting pricing based on the indicated risk factors, and the differences in the probabilities across rows in the table show the effect of changing one demographic characteristic while holding the others constant. ***Statistically different from reference with 99-percent probability; **statistically different from reference with 95-percent probability; *statistically different from reference with 90-percent probability. Green shading (in the gender, family income, age, and region of current residence sections) indicates statistically significant increases from the reference category. Orange shading (in the race section) indicates statistically significant decreases from the reference category.

[a] Gender, age, race, genetic diseases, living in polluted areas, and prior health problems. Analysis run on 5,172 respondent–risk factor combinations.

[b] Illegal drug use, smoking, heavy drinking, and obesity. Analysis run on 3,448 respondent–risk factor combinations.

[c] Analysis run on 6,034 respondent–risk factor combinations.

[d] Analysis run on 4,310 respondent–risk factor combinations.

Individuals in higher-income households also tend to be more supportive of pricing based on risk factors, holding other characteristics constant. The exception is for health risk factors that are less under an individual's control. Here, there is no statistically significant increase in the percentage of higher-income households supporting or strongly supporting higher premiums based on these factors.

Older Americans tend to be more supportive of pricing based on risk factors than younger Americans. The difference is greatest for flood insurance, with the predictive margin showing that 54 percent of Americans aged 65 and older support or strongly support higher premiums when indicated by the flood risk factor versus 40 percent for those aged 18–44. Again, there is no statistically significant difference by age for health risk factors that are less under an individual's control.

The statistically significant negative differences for Black respondents indicate that Black respondents tend to be considerably less supportive of pricing based on risk factors than White respondents. Hispanic respondents do not differ substantially from non-Hispanic respondents in attitudes toward pricing based on risk factors, holding the other demographic characteristics constant.

We found no evidence that the attitudes toward pricing based on risk factors vary depending on whether an individual currently resides in an urban or rural area. We also did not find much evidence of systematic variation by geographic region. The percentages of residents supporting premiums based on risk factors tended to be lowest in the New England and Middle Atlantic region and in the South Central region.[13]

Limitations

Both types of survey questions have their advantages and elicit useful information from respondents. But they also have limitations in addition to those discussed for the first question type above, such as the following:

- Respondents were not told to assume whether the purchase of the specified type of insurance is mandatory. Whether insurance is mandatory or voluntary could conceivably affect the responses.
- The order of the questions could affect responses, but we did not randomly alter the order of the questions when fielding the survey.
- The rate plan options questions are fairly complex, and they might be difficult for some respondents to understand.
- To make questions on whether individuals with specified risk factors should pay more for car insurance easier to understand, we posited changes only in the frequency of the adverse event as opposed to the frequency and severity of the event. Responses could conceivably differ if the questions were framed in terms of expected annual costs (the product of frequency and severity).
- We intentionally did not personalize the questions. For example, in the rate plan options questions, we did not ask the respondent to assume that he or she lived in a low-risk flood area and would have to pay the subsidy to the high-risk homeowners. We did this to avoid having respondents focus on their narrow self-interest and to encourage them to evaluate the desirability of different rating options from a larger social perspective. That said, in a real-world setting in which the low-risk policyholders have to pay the subsidy, support for subsidies might be less than indicated by the survey responses.
- Survey respondents were asked to assume that the specified factor was associated with higher health care or other costs. If respondents were provided with information backing up the assumption, they might be more inclined to accept it for the purposes of the question.

---

[13] The definitions of *urban* and *rural* and the states in each region are listed in Appendix B.

As is the case for any survey, there is always a question of external validity: whether our results reflect actual behavior in the world. While more research using different methods would be useful to buttress our conclusions, we have confidence in our findings for several reasons. First, they are internally logically consistent. We find that respondents' responses are logically coherent and reflect skepticism about risk-based rates in both parts of the survey. In general, the greater control the insured has over the risk, the more support for risk-based pricing. This suggests a coherent belief system that we are observing rather than spurious survey responses. Second, we also observe some consistency between our findings and behavior in the real world. The prohibition on charging individuals more for preexisting conditions was one of the most popular aspects of the Affordable Care Act, for example, while accident-based auto insurance is widely accepted.

CHAPTER 4

Discussion, Policy Implications, and Conclusion

We find that attitudes toward full risk-sharing, partial risk-sharing, and risk-based pricing vary considerably within the U.S. adult population and across insurance settings. Premiums based on individual risk factors are not popular in many settings, and our results suggest that many people are willing to pay considerable amounts to subsidize the insurance premiums of high-risk individuals. This is remarkable and goes against the expectation of Americans' supposedly individualistic nature. It suggests that many citizens view insurance as an institution that should spread risk—for at least some kinds of risk—broadly across individuals.

The results suggest that support for pricing based on individual risk factors is greater when the policyholder has some control over the behavior associated with the higher risk and when the behavior is directly relevant to the risk that is being insured. In the health insurance setting, a majority of the population support higher premiums only in the scenarios we examined when the risk factor associated with higher health care costs is arguably under one's control—i.e., heavy drinking, smoking, and illegal drug use. Although approximately two-thirds of the population support the general concept that flood insurance premiums should be higher for homes at higher flood risk, support falls to less than one-third if increases in flood risk are due to factors beyond the homeowner's control, such as sea level rise or nearby development. In the auto insurance setting, there was support for higher premiums for drivers with more speeding tickets. However, when survey respondents were directed to assume that low credit scores were associated with higher accident rates, few supported higher insurance premiums for this group—perhaps because respondents did not believe that the link between driving behavior and credit scores was sufficiently direct or felt that credit scores are often driven by factors outside the individual's control.

Not only is there strong support for subsidized insurance premiums in many circumstances, but people state that they are willing to pay substantial amounts to support those subsidies. In the case of health insurance premiums for people with leukemia, approximately two-thirds of the population prefer a rate plan in which healthy individuals pay 20 percent ($2,000 per year) more than they would if premiums were strictly based on expected health care costs. Even in a scenario involving an insured individual who drinks heavily, more than 50 percent of the population prefer rate plans in which people who do not drink heavily pay 10 or 20 percent ($1,000 or $2,000 per year) more to premiums that are risk based.

The findings are similar in the flood insurance setting: More than one-half of the population prefer rate plans in which homeowners in low-risk areas pay 100 or 200 percent more ($500 or $1,000 per year) to reduce the premiums of homeowners in high-risk areas. When flood insurance premiums increase in high-risk areas due to sea level rise, 31 percent prefer a plan in which the federal government pays the subsidy, and another 38 percent prefer a plan in which homeowners in low-risk areas pay 100 or 300 percent more to subsidize the premiums in high-risk areas.

Our analysis shows considerable variation across demographic groups in attitudes toward risk-sharing. Men tend to be more in favor of linking premiums to individual risk factors than women, holding the other demographic factors considered in the analysis fixed. Older Americans tend to be more in favor of pricing based on individual risk factors than younger Americans. Individuals in higher-income households also are more in favor of linking premiums to risk than those in lower-income households. Black respondents, in contrast, are less supportive of pricing based on individual risk factors than White respondents, holding other demographic characteristics constant.

Our finding that respondents are more accepting of using risk factors to set insurance prices when the risk factor is more under an individual's control is interesting for both economic and ethical reasons. From an economic perspective, charging risk-based prices in contexts where the individual has some control over the risk is more efficient because it preserves incentives for that individual to reduce the risk. For example, if a driver knows that they will pay more for insurance if they have been involved in car crashes, they have a financial incentive to avoid accidents. They may take various precautions, including driving more carefully, less often, or at safer times.[1] This will reduce the moral hazard associated with insurance— the extent to which an insured individual may alter their behavior because they do not bear the financial consequences of the risk. Whether risk reduction activities are actually undertaken in response to a change in insurance premium (the price elasticity of risk reduction activity) is an interesting empirical question.

There is also an ethical or moral dimension to this finding. Charging higher premiums for a risk factor that someone has no control over seems unfair, even if the factor accurately predicts insured losses. Perhaps the paradigmatic example of this might be the broad consensus that individuals who have a major medical condition should not thereafter be forced to pay higher premiums for health insurance. Any other policy seems cruel if the additional amount that healthy people would be required to pay is relatively low. Our findings suggest that this moral intuition also exists in sectors besides health insurance.

---

[1] For discussion of the continuum of accident prevention methods from short to long run, see James M. Anderson, "The Missing Theory of Variable Selection in the Economic Analysis of Tort Law," *Utah Law Review*, Vol. 2007, No. 2, 2007.

Policy Implications

Our findings have important implications for insurance regulation and public policy. In the auto insurance setting, we found that a low percentage of the population support higher premiums for men, drivers with low credit scores, and drivers in neighborhoods with higher vehicle theft when survey respondents were asked to assume that higher claim costs were associated with these risk factors.[2] In contrast to this finding, all but a handful of states allow insurers to consider these factors in rate-making.[3] This disjuncture may motivate consumer efforts to reform insurance regulatory policies in states where insurers are allowed to consider these factors. Given these findings, insurers and policymakers might wish to restrict the risk factors considered in setting prices to those that are perceived to be more directly within the control of consumers—for example, their driving behavior. Modern telematics (the integration of telecommunications and vehicular technology to wirelessly collect data on performance) make that technologically feasible in a way that was not possible in the recent past; although, of course, driver monitoring raises other concerns. Alternatively, insurers and policymakers may wish to make the case for risk-based pricing directly to consumers through education and by explaining the drawbacks of cross-subsidization.

Our findings in the flood insurance setting also provide insight into the challenges that FEMA faces in moving to risk-based pricing in the NFIP.[4] Although there is considerable support for a rate structure in which premiums for homes in high-risk areas are higher than those in low-risk areas, less than one-third of the population support rates that are fully risk-based. It is thus not unreasonable to expect that the NFIP will face continuing opposition to implementing its new rating methodology. There is even less support for risk-based pricing when premium increases are due to factors beyond the property owner's control, which could well translate into pressure to exempt certain types of properties from risk-based pricing.[5]

Finally, FEMA has been considering flood insurance affordability programs to reduce flood insurance premiums for households with low income and low assets.[6] We found only minority support for a federal subsidy for homeowners whose premiums increase due to sea

---

[2] To be clear, we asked respondents only about the appropriateness of risk-rating by neighborhood, not region or type of environment. So, it is possible that respondents would think that charging less in a rural environment might be acceptable. Indeed, this is purportedly the rationale of the founding of State Farm, which was founded by a farmer who thought that farmers were charged too much for insurance. See Smithsonian National Postal Museum, "State Farm," webpage, September 2016.

[3] See Meyer, undated.

[4] FEMA, "NFIP's Pricing Approach," webpage, undated.

[5] Prior to FEMA's new rating methodology, so-called grandfathering provisions that enabled a property owner to use a prior flood insurance rate map to price a policy are another indicator of the support for subsidies when premiums rise due to factors outside the property owner's control.

[6] See FEMA, *An Affordability Framework for the National Flood Insurance Program*, U.S. Department of Homeland Security, April 17, 2018.

level rise, suggesting challenges in passing the federal legislation needed to establish such a program. However, such assistance was not limited to low-income households in the scenario we presented to respondents. We found that people are more willing to subsize the flood insurance premiums of households with low income and limited assets. Thus, restricting benefits to low-income households could increase support for an affordability program.

The substantial support we found for subsidies raises questions about the potential efficacy of relying on insurance to create incentives to mitigate the effects of natural and other hazards. Risk-based premiums, or premiums close to risk-based premiums, can provide incentives to take action to reduce the vulnerability of individuals or property to natural and other hazards. For example, if flood insurance premiums rise to reflect the increased risk from sea level rise, this may encourage homebuyers to buy properties in areas that are less subject to such risk. However, the considerable popular support for substantial flood insurance subsidies calls into question whether insurance will be able to fulfill its potential to provide appropriate incentives. The pressure we observed to deviate from risk-based premiums is likely to be particularly politically significant when premiums are set by public entities or elected officials. But even when premiums are ostensibly set by private insurers, state regulatory systems that are subject to public pressure might significantly constrain both permissible premiums and the rating factors used. In any case, blind faith in the potential for insurance rates to be a primary tool to incentivize adaptation to climate change and other risks is not likely warranted, at least for personal, as opposed to commercial, lines of insurance.[7]

Several approaches come to mind to address the apparent mismatch between the theoretical benefits of risk-based prices and public sentiment. First, education may help the public understand some of the drawbacks of subsidies and risk-spreading. This may lead to more support for risk-based pricing and the climate change risk mitigation strategies that such pricing incentivizes. Highlighting some of the apparent unfairness of cross-subsidizing a wealthy waterfront landowner's insurance policy, for example, might shift opinions.

Second, rating plans should be considered that move in the direction of risk-based pricing but address some of the fairness and equity considerations. For example, prices might be set at risk-based rates, but targeted assistance could be provided to low-income households under certain circumstances or over limited periods to reduce the burdens of such rates.

---

[7] The point we are making here is not about the extent to which risk-based rates can induce mitigation measures—which is not the issue addressed in this report. The point is that public attitudes may prevent the risk-based prices from being used in the first place.

Finally, further research in the following areas would improve understanding of the public attitudes toward risk-based pricing and their implications for public policy:

- **Impact of personalizing the scenarios.** To encourage respondents to assess trade-offs from a social point of view, we intentionally did not personalize the situations. However, if the survey respondent were presented with a scenario in which they were at low risk and had to pay the subsidy (or, conversely, at high risk and would receive the subsidy), attitudes might differ.

- **Impact of providing additional information on risk factors.** In our survey, respondents were directed to assume that the risk factor under consideration was correlated with expected costs, but no justification was provided for the assertion. It would be useful to understand how the provision of additional information would affect responses. For example, how would statistics on the correlation between credit-based insurance scores and insured losses affect responses?

- **Difference in attitudes when coverage is mandatory.** In our analysis, survey respondents were given no information on whether coverage was mandatory. Support for risk-based pricing could conceivably be lower when coverage is mandatory.

- **Factors driving consumer preferences.** Solicitation of the reasons consumers prefer one rating approach over another would be informative. Relevant factors to consider include the extent to which consumers believe that a risk factor is under an individual's control, the extent to which this consideration entered into their decisions, and whether the households subject to the rate plan are low-income or vulnerable in some other way.

- **More-precise estimates of the subsidy that consumers are willing to pay.** Variation in the partial risk-sharing rating plan posed in the scenarios would provide more-precise estimates of the amount of subsidy that consumers are willing to pay.

- **Use of laboratory experiments to corroborate findings.** Experimental economists may wish to use laboratory experiments to see if our survey-based findings are replicated by using a different methodology.

- **Quantitative analysis of the real-world inefficiencies and lost consumer welfare attributable to cross-subsidies.** Such analysis would be useful to policymakers wrestling with how to trade off efficiency and equity considerations.

Conclusion

Policy analysts, economists, and lawyers often focus on efficiency as a key, if not paramount, goal in thinking about how insurance can be regulated to maximize welfare. Our findings suggest that American consumers have broader concerns.[8] Whether these are a function of ignorance about the drawbacks of insurance cross-subsidization or well-reasoned normative beliefs about trade-offs between efficiency and equity is difficult to ascertain. Most likely, they are a combination of both. But insurers and insurance policymakers ignore these beliefs at their peril. Otherwise, they may find significant political opposition to policy proposals that appear otherwise attractive.

---

[8] Property insurance is, of course, only one social mechanism for redistributing loss. Tort law is another. Our findings may therefore have relevance to debates in tort law about the extent to which tort liability is justified by its insurance function—serving as a means of compensating individuals for certain kinds of losses. Critics of this view of tort reasonably criticize it for its expense and inefficiency. But that may be missing the point. In the insurance context, we found support for significant redistribution between high-risk and low-risk policyholders. This suggests an appetite for redistribution that might apply to tort law as well and, indeed, is reflected in trial lawyer wisdom about the appeal of a sympathetic plaintiff facing a deep-pocketed defendant. Better understanding how our findings apply in the tort law context would be a productive avenue for further research.

Survey Instrument

The complete list of survey questions is reproduced in this appendix. In each case, we asked respondents to assume that the risk factor in question is associated with higher losses. We did so to focus the respondent on the fairness of charging more for the risk rather than speculating about the actual relationship between the risk factor in question and the underlying risk.

Question 1_1
Homeowners can buy insurance that covers losses due to flooding. There is debate over whether the cost should vary depending on the flood risk of the home being insured.

Do you think a homeowner should pay more for flood insurance if:

	Strongly Support (1)	Support (2)	Neither Support nor Oppose (3)	Oppose (4)	Strongly Oppose (5)
The home is at higher risk of flooding than other homes? (1)	○	○	○	○	○
The home is at higher risk of flooding than other homes, but the household has low income and limited assets? (2)	○	○	○	○	○
The homeowner has lived in the home for many years and flood risk recently increased due to sea level rise? (3)	○	○	○	○	○
The homeowner has lived in the home for many years and flood risk recently increased due to nearby development? (4)	○	○	○	○	○
There has been prior flood damage at the property suggesting greater risk of future flooding? (5)	○	○	○	○	○

Question 1_2

Likewise, there is much debate about whether health insurance cost should vary across individuals with different health profiles.

	Strongly Support (1)	Support (2)	Neither Support nor Oppose (3)	Oppose (4)	Strongly Oppose (5)
Assume that annual health care costs are higher for women. Do you think that women should pay more for health insurance? (1)	O	O	O	O	O
Assume that annual health care costs are higher for certain races. Do you think that people of these races should pay more for health insurance? (2)	O	O	O	O	O
Assume that annual health care costs are higher for older people. Do you think that older people should pay more for health insurance? (3)	O	O	O	O	O
Assume that annual health care costs are higher for people with certain genetic diseases. Do you think that people with these genetic diseases should pay more for health insurance? (4)	O	O	O	O	O
Assume that annual health care costs are higher for heavy drinkers. Do you think that heavy drinkers should pay more for health insurance? (5)	O	O	O	O	O
Assume that annual health care costs are higher for illegal drug users. Do you think that illegal drug users should pay more for health insurance? (6)	O	O	O	O	O
Assume that annual health care costs are higher for smokers. Do you think that smokers should pay more for health insurance? (7)	O	O	O	O	O
Assume that annual health care costs are higher for people who are obese. Do you think that people who are obese should pay more for health insurance? (8)	O	O	O	O	O
Assume that annual health care costs are higher for people with prior health problems such as asthma, diabetes, or cancer. Do you think that people with prior health problems should pay more for health insurance? (9)	O	O	O	O	O
Assume that annual health care costs are higher for people who live in heavily polluted areas. Do you think that people who live in heavily polluted areas should pay more for health insurance? (10)	O	O	O	O	O

Question 1_3

In return for a fixed annual or monthly payment, term life insurance pays a set amount to the beneficiaries if the policyholder dies during the period covered by the policy. A typical term for such a policy is 20 years.

	Strongly Support (1)	Support (2)	Neither Support nor Oppose (3)	Oppose (4)	Strongly Oppose (5)
Assume that the chance of dying during the policy period is higher for men. Do you think that men should pay more for life insurance? (1)	O	O	O	O	O
Assume that the chance of dying during the policy period is higher for certain races. Do you think that people of these races should pay more for life insurance? (2)	O	O	O	O	O
Assume that the chance of dying during the policy period is higher for older people. Do you think that older people should pay more for life insurance? (3)	O	O	O	O	O
Assume that the chance of dying during the policy period is higher for people with certain genetic diseases. Do you think that people with these genetic diseases should pay more for life insurance? (4)	O	O	O	O	O
Assume that the chance of dying during the policy period is higher for heavy drinkers. Do you think that heavy drinkers should pay more for life insurance? (5)	O	O	O	O	O
Assume that the chance of dying during the policy period is higher for illegal drug users. Do you think that illegal drug users should pay more for life insurance? (6)	O	O	O	O	O
Assume that the chance of dying during the policy period is higher for smokers. Do you think that smokers should pay more for life insurance? (7)	O	O	O	O	O
Assume that the chance of dying during the policy period is higher for people who are obese. Do you think that people who are obese should pay more for life insurance? (8)	O	O	O	O	O
Assume that the chance of dying during the policy period is higher for people with prior health problems such as asthma, diabetes, or cancer. Do you think that people with prior health problems should pay more for life insurance? (9)	O	O	O	O	O
Assume that the chance of dying during the policy period is higher for people who live in heavily polluted areas. Do you think that people who live in heavily polluted areas should pay more for life insurance? (10)	O	O	O	O	O

Question 1_4
The final question in this section asks your opinion regarding how the cost of car insurance should vary depending on factors that can affect the chance of causing an accident or of a car being stolen.

	Strongly Support (1)	Support (2)	Neither Support nor Oppose (3)	Oppose (4)	Strongly Oppose (5)
Assume that the chance of causing an accident is higher for younger drivers. Should younger drivers pay more for car insurance? (1)	O	O	O	O	O
Assume that the chance of causing an accident is higher for drivers with more speeding tickets. Should drivers with more speeding tickets pay more for car insurance? (2)	O	O	O	O	O
Assume that the chance of causing an accident is higher for people who drive faster cars. Should people who drive faster cars pay more for car insurance? (3)	O	O	O	O	O
Assume that the chance of causing an accident is higher for drivers with low credit scores. Should drivers with low credit scores pay more for car insurance? (4)	O	O	O	O	O
Assume that the chance of causing an accident is higher for men. Should men pay more for car insurance? (5)	O	O	O	O	O
Assume that the chance of causing an accident is higher for people of certain races. Should people of certain races pay more for car insurance? (6)	O	O	O	O	O
Assume that the chance of a vehicle being stolen is higher in certain neighborhoods. Should drivers who live in these neighborhoods pay more for car insurance? (7)	O	O	O	O	O

Question 2_1

John has a type of leukemia that requires regular medical monitoring and treatment. If the amount he is required to pay for health insurance were set to equal his expected medical costs during the policy period, John would pay $30,000 per year. The expected medical costs for a healthy person John's age are $10,000 per year.

Insurers and insurance regulators are considering different approaches for pricing health insurance coverage. In Plan A, each person pays their risk-based premium. In Plan B, the risk is spread across all people covered by the insurance. In Plan C, there is some risk sharing across the policyholders.

Insurance Rating Category	Percent of Population	Plan A: Risk-Based Insurance Premium	Plan B: Equal Insurance Premium	Plan C: Partial Risk-Sharing
People with leukemia John's age	10%	$30,000	$12,000	$20,000
Healthy people John's age	90%	$10,000	$12,000	$11,000

Which plan do you prefer? Please rank the plans with "1" indicating your first choice, "2" indicating your second choice, and "3" indicating your third choice. This example assumes there are 9 healthy people for each person with leukemia, and insurance "premium" refers to the amount John pays for his health insurance.

To enter ranking, click plans in order of preference. To change rankings, re-click option(s).
_____ Plan A: Risk-Based Insurance Premium (1)
_____ Plan B: Equal Insurance Premium (2)
_____ Plan C: Partial Risk Sharing (3)

Question 2_2

Now instead of leukemia, assume that John has drunk heavily for many years. Heavy drinking has been shown to be associated with higher lifetime health care costs. Again, the proposed plans are constructed assuming heavy drinkers make up 10% of the population.

Insurance Rating Category	Percent of Population	Plan A: Risk-Based Insurance Premium	Plan B: Equal Insurance Premium	Plan C: Partial Risk Sharing
People who drink heavily and are John's age	10%	$30,000	$12,000	$20,000
Premium for healthy people John's age	90%	$10,000	$12,000	$11,000

Which plan do you now prefer? Please rank the programs with "1" indicating your first choice, "2" indicating your second choice, and "3" indicating your third choice.

To enter ranking, click plans in order of preference. To change rankings, re-click option(s).
_____ Plan A: Risk-Based Premium (1)
_____ Plan B: Equal Premium (2)
_____ Plan C: Partial Risk Sharing (3)

Question 2_3

Imagine a town which sometimes floods. The flood risk varies considerably across the town. If insurance premiums reflect the flood risk at each home,
- the cost of flood insurance for a home in the low-risk areas of the town would be $500 per year,
- the cost for a similar home in the high-risk areas would be $2,500 per year,
- the average premium across the whole town would be $1,500 per year.

There are equal numbers of homes in the low-risk and high-risk parts of this community.

Insurers and insurance regulators are considering different approaches for pricing insurance coverage, and insurance "premium" refers to the amount the homeowner pays for flood insurance.
- In Plan A, each homeowner pays the risk-based premium for his or her home
- In Plan B, the risk is spread across all homes in the town
- In Plan C, there is some risk sharing across the town.

Insurance Rating Category	Percent of Homes in Community	Plan A: Risk-Based Premium	Plan B: Equal Premium	Plan C: Partial Risk-Sharing
Homes in low-risk areas	50%	$500	$1,500	$1,000
Homes in high-risk areas	50%	$2,500	$1,500	$2,000

Which plan do you prefer? Please rank the programs with "1" indicating your first choice, "2" indicating your second choice, and "3" indicating your third choice.

To enter ranking, click plans in order of preference. To change rankings, re-click option(s).

____ Plan A: Risk-Based Insurance Premium (1)
____ Plan B: Equal Insurance Premium (2)
____ Plan C: Partial Risk Sharing (3)

Question 2_4

Insurers and insurance regulators decide to go with Plan A in the previous question; thus, the premium in the low-risk areas is $500 and the premium in the high-risk areas is $2,500.

Ten years later, the same people are living in each home, but sea level rise has caused flood risk to increase in the high-risk areas. If insurance premiums reflect flood risk at each home, the premium in the high-risk areas would now be $3,500 and the premium in the low-risk areas would remain at $500.

Insurers and regulators are now considering the following new plans. The first three plans are similar to those you saw in the previous question. The fourth plan provides a subsidy for the homeowners in the high-risk area. The subsidy would require the federal government to increase tax revenue enough to cover the overall amount paid in subsidies.

Insurance Rating Category	Percent of Homes in Community	Plan D: Risk-Based Premium	Plan E: Equal Premium	Plan F: Partial Risk-Sharing	Plan G: Federal Subsidy
Homes in low-risk areas	50%	$500	$2,000	$1,000	$500
Homes in high-risk areas	50%	$3,500	$2,000	$3,000	$2,500
Subsidy paid by federal taxpayers for each home in the high-risk area		0	0	0	$1,000

Which plan do you prefer? Please rank the programs with "1" indicating your first choice, "2" indicating your second choice, "3" indicating your third choice, and "4" indicating your fourth choice.

To enter ranking, click plans in order of preference. To change rankings, re-click option(s).
   ____ Plan D: Risk-Based Premium (1)
   ____ Plan E: Equal Premium (2)
   ____ Plan F: Partial Risk Sharing (3)
   ____ Plan G: Federal Subsidy (4)

Question 2_5

Insurers and insurance regulators are leaning toward a subsidy for homeowners in the high-risk areas that are facing the higher risk due to sea level rise and are considering which homeowners in the high-risk areas should receive the subsidy. If fewer households receive the subsidy, there would be less burden on federal taxpayers.

Which of the following is the best approach, in your opinion? Please rank the approaches with "1" indicating your first choice,"2" indicating your second choice, and "3" indicating your third choice.

_____ All homeowners in the high-risk areas should receive the subsidy, which would reduce their premium from $3,500 to $2,500. (1)

_____ All homeowners in the high-risk areas should receive a subsidy, but the amount of the subsidy should be less for those households with higher incomes or substantial assets. (2)

_____ Only those homeowners with incomes and assets below a certain level should receive the subsidy. (3)

Question 3_1

What hazards are you concerned about in your area?
Check all that apply.

❑ Flood (1)

❑ Hurricane (2)

❑ Tornado (3)

❑ Strong wind (4)

❑ Earthquake (5)

❑ Wildfire (6)

❑ Terrorism (7)

❑ Landslide (8)

❑ Hail (9)

❑ Ice storm (10)

❑ Other, Specify: (11)_____ [Other]

Respondent Characteristics

The demographics of the survey respondents, both before and after weighting, are provided in Table B.1.

TABLE B.1

Demographics of Survey Respondents

Characteristic	Unweighted (%)	Weighted (%)
Family income[a]		
<$35,000	24.3	23.3
≥$35,000 and <$60,000	23.2	21.9
≥$60,000 and <$100,000	23.8	23.7
≥$100,000	28.7	31.2
Gender		
Female	57.1	51.7
Male	42.9	48.3
Race[b]		
White	77.7	73.7
Black	9.2	12.0
American Indian/Alaska Native	1.7	2.1
Asian or Pacific Islander	3.1	3.7
Other	7.4	8.4
Ethnicity		
Not Hispanic	85.1	83.7
Hispanic	14.9	16.3
Age		
18–44	35.5	45.9
45–64	33.0	31.9
≥65	31.5	22.1

Table B.1—Continued

Characteristic	Unweighted (%)	Weighted (%)
Housing tenure		
Own	71.2	68.6
Rent	28.8	31.4
Flood concern		
No	69.0	68.9
Yes	31.0	31.1
Urban/rural[b,c]		
Rural	22.5	26.5
Urban	77.4	73.4
Unknown	0.1	0.1
Region of current residence[b]		
New England and Middle Atlantic	17.9	19.9
South Atlantic	18.7	19.9
North Central	17.0	16.2
South Central	17.1	17.4
Mountain	11.3	12.2
Pacific	18.0	14.5
Unknown	0.1	0.1

SOURCE: Authors' analysis of survey responses.

NOTE: Based on 867 responses unless otherwise noted.

[a] Based on 864 responses.

[b] Based on 866 responses.

[c] *Rural* refers to a rural or small town with a population less than 50,000. *Urban* refers to a small to midsize city or a large city with a population of more than 50,000. The classification is based on the U.S. Census definition, and survey respondents are classified using current zip code.

Statistical Methods

In this appendix, we describe the statistical methods used to produce the estimates in this analysis. We also report statistical confidence intervals for the findings presented in Figures 3.1 through 3.4.

Method Used to Estimate the Proportion of the U.S. Population Favoring Various Pricing Approaches

As discussed in Chapter 2, we conducted the survey using RAND's ALP. When relaying the survey responses to the authors, ALP staff also provided survey weights for each observation. These weights were generated using a ranking algorithm to match the ALP to the adult U.S. population, measured using the Current Population Survey. The weights match on four bivariate discrete distributions: gender by age, gender by race and ethnicity, gender by highest education, and family income by adult household size.

We used Stata's svy command infrastructure to estimate population estimates from the survey responses. The weights are set in Stata as "pweights," and the weighted proportions are calculated using "svy: proportion <variable name>."

The first column of Table C.1 shows the estimate of the percentage of the U.S. adult population that supports or strongly supports higher premiums for policyholders with each of indicated risk factors. The 95-percent confidence interval is provided in the last two columns.

TABLE C.1

Confidence Intervals for Estimates Reported in Figures 3.1 Through 3.4

Insurance Line and Risk Factor	Percentage Who Support or Strongly Support	95-Percent Confidence Interval	
		Lower Bound	Upper Bound
Health insurance			
Women	10.8	8.1	14.2
Races with higher health care costs	6.3	4.6	8.4
Older people	7.9	5.8	10.6
People with certain genetic diseases	5.7	4.0	8.2
Heavy drinkers	53.9	48.0	59.0
Illegal drug users	59.6	54.0	65.0
Smokers	58.5	53.0	64.0
People who are obese	29.6	25.0	34.0
People with prior health problems	6.4	4.5	9.0
People who live in heavily polluted areas	6.3	4.1	9.6
Term life insurance			
Women	16.4	13.5	20.0
Races with higher health care costs	8.8	6.8	11.3
Older people	21.2	17.3	25.9
People with certain genetic diseases	13.2	10.4	16.5
Heavy drinkers	53.8	48.2	59.3
Illegal drug users	58.3	52.6	63.8
Smokers	60.6	55.3	65.6
People who are obese	34.4	29.7	39.5
People with prior health problems	13.9	11.1	17.1
People who live in heavily polluted areas	10.2	7.6	13.7
Auto insurance			
Younger drivers	58.5	52.8	64.0
More speeding tickets	81.7	77.4	85.4
Drivers of faster cars	46.1	40.6	51.7
Lower credit scores	9.9	7.4	13.1
Men	16.3	13.3	19.8
People of races that cause more accidents	7.5	5.5	10.0

Table C.1—Continued

Insurance Line and Risk Factor	Percentage Who Support or Strongly Support	95-Percent Confidence Interval	
		Lower Bound	Upper Bound
Neighborhoods with higher vehicle theft	18.5	15.1	22.4
Flood insurance			
Home at higher risk of flooding	65.9	60.8	70.7
Higher risk, but low income, limited assets	36.7	31.3	42.3
Long time in home but risk is higher due to sea level rise	33.0	28.3	38.0
Long time in home but risk is higher due to nearby development	22.4	18.2	27.2
Prior flood damage suggesting greater risk	60.2	54.4	65.7

SOURCE: Authors' analysis of survey responses.

Statistical Methods Used in Demographic Analysis

The variation in support for pricing based on individual risk factors across demographic groups is estimated using the following relationship:

$$Prob\left(support_{if}\right) = f\left(factor_f; characteristics_i\right),$$

where

i = survey respondent

f = categorical variable for risk factor f

$support_{if}$ = indicator of whether the respondent i supports or strongly supports higher premiums for risk factor f

$factor_f$ = categorical variable for risk factor f

$characteristics_i$ = categorical variables for each of the demographic characteristics considered.

Relationship (1) is estimated using Stata's logit command, with respondent support being the positive outcome. The "vce(cluster <respondent ID>)" option is used to account for multiple observations for the same respondent. The "vce" option specifies how to estimate the variance-covariance matrix corresponding to the parameter estimates. It affects the calculated standard errors of the estimates but not the parameter estimates. The observations are not weighted in this analysis. The predictive margins reported in Table 3.6 are calculated using "margins <variable>."

Additional Analysis of Responses to Survey Questions on Rate Plans

In this appendix, we provide additional analysis on the survey responses to questions that ask participants to rank different rating plans. We then examine the sensitivity of the findings in Chapter 3 to excluding types of responses that could indicate that the respondent did not fully understand the question.

Responses to Questions 2_1, 2_2, and 2_3 are shown in Table D.1 for each of the possible rate plan ranking permutations. In Permutation 1, the ranking falls as the subsidy increases. In Permutation 2, the ranking rises as the subsidy increases. Considering respondent-specific social welfare functions in which each respondent weighs the equity and efficiency of each rating plan, Permutation 1 is consistent with a social welfare function that monotonically decreases as the subsidy increases (see Welfare Function 1 in Figure D.1). However, it is also consistent with a welfare function that peaks at a subsidy level somewhere between the risk-based pricing and partial risk-sharing plans presented to survey respondents (see Welfare Function 2 in Figure D.1). Similarly, Permutation 2 is consistent with a social welfare function that monotonically increases as the subsidy increases or peaks somewhere between partial risk-sharing and full risk-sharing.

TABLE D.1

Tabulation of Responses for Questions That Ask Respondents to Rank Rating Plans

Ranking Permutation	Rank			Percentage of U.S. Adult Population		
	First	Second	Third	Leukemia Scenario (Question 2_1)	Heavy-Drinking Scenario (Question 2_2)	Flood Insurance Scenario (Question 2_3)
1	Risk BP	Partial RS	Full RS	5	31	35
2	Full RS	Partial RS	Risk BP	49	28	21
3	Partial RS	Risk BP	Full RS	5	7	7
4	Partial RS	Full RS	Risk BP	16	12	16
5	Risk BP	Full RS	Partial RS	4	11	10
6	Full RS	Risk BP	Partial RS	9	5	7
7	Incomplete ranking but risk BP first	N/A	N/A	1	2	1
8	Incomplete ranking but partial RS first	N/A	N/A	2	1	1
9	Incomplete ranking but full RS first	N/A	N/A	8	3	3
10	No response	N/A	N/A	1	1	1
Total	N/A	N/A	N/A	100	100	100

SOURCE: Authors' analysis of survey responses.

NOTE: Full RS = full risk-sharing; partial RS = partial risk-sharing; risk BP = risk-based pricing; N/A = not applicable.

Ranking Permutations 3 and 4 are consistent with a welfare function with an interior peak (see Figure D.2). Permutations 5 and 6 are consistent with a welfare function with an interior trough—that is, the two extremes in terms of subsidy (risk-based pricing and full risk-sharing) are preferred to a rating plan in the middle (partial risk-sharing). As can be seen in Table D.1, between 13 and 17 percent of responses fall into these categories.

FIGURE D.1

Examples of Social Welfare Functions Consistent with Ranking Permutation 1

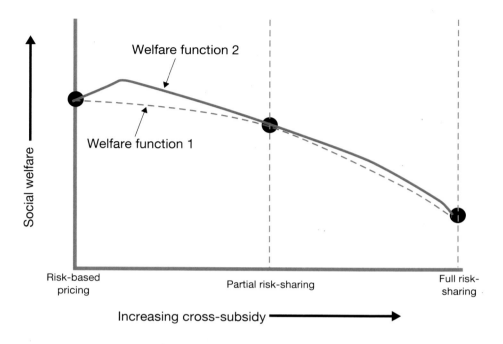

FIGURE D.2

Examples of Social Welfare Functions Consistent with Ranking Permutation 3

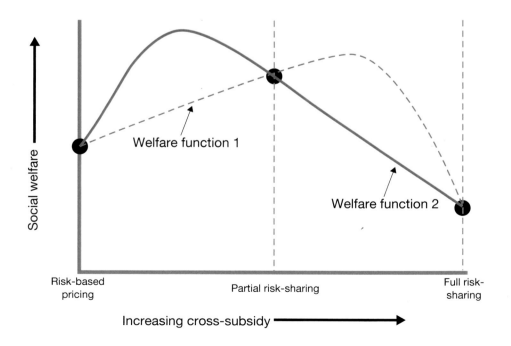

The analysis of the ranking permutations in Table D.1 provides some insight into the range in which the preferred level of subsidy falls. Consider the flood insurance scenario (the last column of Table D.1), and assume that the social welfare function for each individual is either monotonic or has a single peak. The ranges in which the implied preferred subsidy falls are shown in Table D.2. If Permutation 1 is selected, the peak of the social welfare function could fall anywhere between the risk-based pricing and the partial risk-sharing options. We can conclude the same for Permutation 7—assuming that partial risk-sharing would be ranked second and full risk-sharing third. Thus, we can infer that 36 percent of the U.S. adult population would prefer that low-risk policyholders pay a subsidy somewhere between $0 and $500 per year (adding the percentages selecting Permutations 1 and 7 in Table D.1).

TABLE D.2

Implied Range of Preferred Subsidies by Scenario

| Ranking Permutation | Rank | | | Range for Preferred Subsidy[a] | |
	First	Second	Third	Health Scenarios (Questions 2_1 and 2_2)	Flood Insurance Scenario (Question 2_3)
1	Risk BP	Partial RS	Full RS	[0, 1,000)	[0, 500)
2	Full RS	Partial RS	Risk BP	(1,000, 2,000]	(500, 1,000]
3	Partial RS	Risk BP	Full RS	(0, 2,000)	(0, 1,000)
4	Partial RS	Full RS	Risk BP	(0, 2,000)	(0, 1,000)
5	Risk BP	Full RS	Partial RS	Could not be determined	Could not be determined
6	Full RS	Risk BP	Partial RS	Could not be determined	Could not be determined
7	Incomplete ranking but risk BP first	N/A	N/A	[0, 1,000)[b]	[0, 500)[b]
8	Incomplete ranking but partial RS first	N/A	N/A	(0, 2,000)	(0, 1,000)
9	Incomplete ranking but full RS first	N/A	N/A	(1,000, 2,000][c]	(500, 1,000][c]
10	No response	N/A	N/A	Missing	Missing

SOURCE: Authors' analysis of survey responses,

NOTE: Assumes that social welfare functions for each individual are monotonic or have a single peak. Risk BP = risk-based pricing; partial RS = partial risk-sharing; full RS = full risk-sharing; N/A = not applicable.

[a] A bracket indicates that the endpoint is included in the interval. A parenthesis indicates that the endpoint is not included in interval.

[b] Assumes that partial risk-sharing would be ranked second and full risk-sharing third.

[c] Assumes that partial risk-sharing would be ranked second and risk-based pricing third.

Analogously, combining Permutations 2 and 8, 22 percent would prefer a subsidy somewhere between $500 and $1,000. Permutations 3, 4, and 9 (26 percent of the adult population) do not provide any information on the range in which the preferred subsidy would fall—with a single-peaked social welfare function, the preferred subsidy could fall anywhere in the range of subsidies spanned by the plans offered.

Permutations 5 and 6 are inconsistent with an assumption that preferences are either monotonic or single-peaked.[1] We thus are unable to infer the preferred subsidy level for the 13–17 percent of survey participants who responded in this way without making stronger assumptions that we cannot justify.

Using this analysis, we can develop a lower bound and potential upper estimate for the percentage of the U.S. adult population supporting substantial subsidies in each scenario. The lower bound is the sum of the proportions of the population indicating Permutations 2 and 9. A possible upper estimate is the percentage of population who could support the substantial subsidy level, excluding responses that likely do not provide useful information (the sum of Permutations 2, 3, 4, 8, and 9 divided by (100 – the sum of Permutations 5, 6, and 10). Namely,

- **Leukemia scenario (Question 2_1):** At least 57 percent of the U.S. adult population prefer a subsidy between $1,000 and $2,000. The percentage could be as high as 93 percent.
- **Heavy-drinking scenario (Question 2_2):** At least 31 percent of the U.S. adult population prefer a subsidy between $1,000 and $2,000. The percentage could be as high as 61 percent.
- **Flood insurance scenario (Question 2_3):** At least 24 percent of the U.S. adult population prefer a subsidy between $500 and $1,000. The percentage could be as high as 59 percent.

The upper estimate is quite unlikely, given that a number of uncertainties are resolved in favor of the higher estimate, and is so high as to not be particularly useful. This exercise shows the limits of using a survey question design with three rating plans to estimate the percentage of the population who prefer various subsidy levels. Additional survey work testing a range of partial rate-sharing plans would provide greater precision on the distribution of preferences.

To investigate the sensitivity of the results in Table 3.3 to excluding observations with nonsensible rate plan rankings, we compare the estimates of the percentage of the population preferring each of the rating plans in the heavy-drinking scenario (Question 2_2) with and without respondents who answered with ranking Permutations 5 and 6. Table D.3 shows that the percentage preferring risk-based pricing falls somewhat, but the results are not a great deal different.

---

[1] It could be that some of the respondents who answered in this way did not fully understand the question.

TABLE D.3

Effect of Excluding Responses of Respondents with Nonsensible Rating Plan Rankings: Heavy-Drinking Scenario

Rate Plan	Including All Responses		Excluding Respondents Who Answered with Ranking Permutations 5 and 6	
	Percentage of Population Preferring Plan	95-Percent Confidence Interval	Percentage of Population Preferring Plan	95-Percent Confidence Interval
Risk-based pricing	44	[38, 49]	39	[34, 45]
Partial risk-sharing	20	[16, 25]	23	[19, 30]
Full risk-sharing	36	[31, 42]	37	[31, 43]

SOURCE: Authors' analysis of survey responses.

Bibliography

Abraham, Kenneth S., *Distributing Risk: Insurance, Legal Theory, and Public Policy*, Yale University Press, 1986.

Abraham, Kenneth S., *The Liability Century: Insurance and Tort Law from the Progressive Era to 9/11*, Harvard University Press, 2008.

Anderson, James M. "The Missing Theory of Variable Selection in the Economic Analysis of Tort Law," *Utah Law Review*, Vol. 2007, No. 2, 2007.

Baker, Tom, "Where's the Insurance in Mass Tort Litigation?" *Texas Law Review*, Vol. 101, No. 7, 2023.

Buchmueller, Thomas, and John DiNardo, "Did Community Rating Induce an Adverse Selection Death Spiral? Evidence from New York, Pennsylvania, and Connecticut," *American Economic Review*, Vol. 92, No. 1, March 2002.

Calabresi, Guido, "Some Thoughts on Risk Distribution and the Law of Torts," *Yale Law Journal,* Vol. 70, No. 4, 1961.

Einav, Liran, Amy Finkelstein, and Neale Mahoney, "Chapter 14 - The IO of Selection Markets," in Kate Ho, Ali Hortaçsu, and Alessandro Lizzer, eds., *Handbook of Industrial Organization*, Vol. 5, Elsevier, 2021.

Federal Emergency Management Agency, "NFIP's Pricing Approach," webpage, undated. As of February 20, 2024:
https://www.fema.gov/flood-insurance/risk-rating

Federal Emergency Management Agency, *An Affordability Framework for the National Flood Insurance Program*, U.S. Department of Homeland Security, April 17, 2018.

FEMA—*See* Federal Emergency Management Agency.

Geistfeld, Mark A., "Risk Distribution and the Law of Torts: Carrying Calabresi Further," *Law and Contemporary Problems*, Vol. 77, No. 2, 2014.

Hanson, Jon D., and Kyle D. Logue, "The First-Party Insurance Externality: An Economic Justification for Enterprise Liability," *Cornell Law Review*, Vol. 76, No. 1, 1990.

Heller, Douglas, and Michelle Styczynski, *Major Auto Insurers Raise Rates Based on Economic Factors: Low- and Moderate-Income Drivers Charged Higher Premiums*, Consumer Federation of America, June 27, 2016.

Insurance Information Institute, "Background on: Insurance Scoring," in *Online Insurance Handbook*, undated.

Insurance Information Institute, *Trends and Insights: Risk-Based Pricing of Insurance*, September 2022.

James, Fleming, Jr., "Contribution Among Joint Tortfeasors: A Pragmatic Criticism," *Harvard Law Review*, Vol. 54, 1941.

Kiviat, Barbara, "Which Data Fairly Differentiate? American Views on the Use of Personal Data in Two Market Settings," *Sociological Science*, Vol. 8, January 2021.

Meyer, Susan, "Car Insurance Rating Factors by State: What Information Can Car Insurance Companies Use to Price Car Insurance Rates? And How Does That Vary by State?" The Zebra, webpage, undated. As of March 27, 2023:
https://www.thezebra.com/resources/research/car-insurance-rating-factors-by-state/

Pollard, Michael S., and Matthew D. Baird, *The RAND American Life Panel: Technical Description*, RAND Corporation, RR-1651, 2017. As of May 21, 2024:
https://www.rand.org/pubs/research_reports/RR1651.html

Powell, Lars, "Risk-Based Pricing of Property and Liability Insurance," *Journal of Insurance Regulation*, Vol. 39, No. 4, 2020.

Priest, George L., "The Invention of Enterprise Liability: A Critical History of the Intellectual Foundations of Modern Tort Law," *Journal of Legal Studies*, Vol. 14, No. 3, December 1985.

RAND Corporation, "About the American Life Panel," webpage, undated. As of April 1, 2024:
https://www.rand.org/education-and-labor/survey-panels/alp/about.html

Smithsonian National Postal Museum, "State Farm," webpage, September 2016. As of May 22, 2024:
https://postalmuseum.si.edu/exhibition/
america's-mailing-industry-industry-segments-financial-services-industry/state-farm